W9-CLM-857

Paths to Prayer

Robert F. Morneau

ST. ANTHONY MESSENGER PRESS

Cincinnati, Ohio

Scripture citations are taken from the *New Revised Standard Version of the Bible*, copyright ©1989 by the Division of Christian Education of the National Council of the Churches of Christ in the USA. Used by permission. All rights reserved.

Excerpts from the English translation of the *Catechism of the Catholic Church* for use in the United States of America, copyright ©1994, United States Catholic Conference, Inc.— Libreria Editrice Vaticana. Used with permission.

"Doxology" reprinted from *Selected Poetry of Jessica Powers*, edited by Regina Siegfried and Robert Morneau. Copyright ©1989 by Carmelite Monastery of Pewaukee, Wisconsin. Reprinted by permission of the publisher, Sheed & Ward.

Cover illustration by Natalie Cox Jaynes
Cover design by Mary Alfieri
Electronic pagination and format by Sandy L. Digman
ISBN 0-86716-326-7

Published by St. Anthony Messenger Press
Printed in the U.S.A.

Contents

Acknowledgments

There are four people who have used red ink in bringing these twelve articles into their present form. I am indebted to Sister Mary de Sales Hoffmann, O.S.F., Sister Marie Isabel McElrone, O.S.F., Father Jeremy Harrington, O.F.M., and John Bookser Feister for their editorial skills and patient support.

Preface

With a slight jar to the memory we might be able to recall who it was that first taught us how to ride a bicycle, how to bow-tie a shoe string, how to form our letters—and indeed, how to pray. The disciples of Jesus one day asked: "Lord, tell us how to pray." Embedded deep in their memory, deep in their souls, was the Lord's Prayer.

As Christians and disciples we hear three fundamental calls in the gospel: pray, fast, give alms. By responding to these gospel imperatives, we follow the path that Jesus trod. Discipleship is not possible if we neglect the needs of others, if we do not embrace the cross by means of appropriate self-denial, if we do not communicate on a regular basis with God.

One of the difficulties in speaking about prayer is that each person's experience is unique. No two people pray exactly the same way; no two people have identical experiences of God; no two people have the same vocabulary or disposition to silence. Sweeping generalizations regarding prayer life are impossible. We enter God's presence alone, with all of our graces and sins. The beauty is that God takes us just as we are and speaks to our heart.

Two years ago I received a call from Father Jeremy Harrington, O.F.M., publisher of St. Anthony Messenger Press. He had a request: Would I be willing to write twelve articles on the topic of prayer, using as a basis the fourth section of the *Catechism of the Catholic Church*? I quickly attempted to conjure up reasons why my schedule and characteristic inertia would allow for a negative response. But Father Harrington was persistent and persuasive. As I hung up after that fateful call, I had twelve term papers to do, each consisting of 2910 words.

In the end it proved to be a both a fateful and a fortunate call. Now I was committed to an intense reading and study of the *Catechism*, as well as figuring out ways of rendering its message as pastoral as possible.

The *Catechism of the Catholic Church* is divided into four sections. Part One deals with the profession of faith; Part Two with the celebration of the Christian mystery, our sacramental life; the third section is concerned with our life in Christ, our vocation to live in the Holy Spirit; and the fourth part summarizes our tradition regarding Christian prayer. This carefully crafted text is an outstanding resource of our Catholic heritage and deserves serious and prayerful study. St. Anthony Messenger Press is to be commended for assisting in the implementation of this major document.

As the *Catechism* clearly points out, our Catholic tradition is rich in the forms and varieties of prayer. Prayer can be private or public, verbal or silent, filled with praise or begging for mercy. Regardless of style, prayer is always to be holistic, involving the mind, heart and hands. It is also to be inclusive, in that prayer embraces all of creation as we attempt to respond to a God who continually blesses us and calls us to full maturity.

The *Catechism of the Catholic Church* provides us with a thorough summary and magnificent overview of prayer in the Catholic tradition. The twelve essays in this book attempt to apply the *Catechism*'s theology to our everyday life. The reader is encouraged to return time and again to the primary source, the *Catechism*, for further reflection.

The overarching theme of this book is "paths to prayer." The Christian life is a journey and along the path of our communal life we are called to serve and to pray. Chronology was of no major significance in the ordering of the topics. This is not to say, however, that there was no method in this madness.

God's revelation is somewhat thunderous (quiet, too, at times) and our response, according to the poet George Herbert, is "reversed thunder." Chapter One, "Prayer: 'Reversed Thunder'" is a reflection on the nature of prayer, with a challenge to the reader to memorize prayers by Dag Hammarskjöld and Saint Richard of Chichester.

Every spiritual exercise, be it works of mercy, Scripture reading, asceticism or prayer, has certain principles and guidelines that keep us on the gospel road. Chapter Two deals with five principles of prayer that point the way toward union with God. The essential principle is that God always takes the initiative on our journey of faith.

Principles tend to manifest themselves in specific habits, patterned activity that achieves desired results.

Prayerful people develop certain virtues by which they enter and remain in the presence of God. Our third chapter, "Seven Habits of Prayerful People," lists habits such as, "act truthfully," "persevere," "keep watch," whereby we foster intimacy with our Triune God.

Pragmatism is treasured in our society. We like to see things get done. Thus we draw up job descriptions outlining the specific tasks that make up our professions. Though prayer is ultimately a relationship, there is a kind of pragmatic technology involved in how we pray, as will be seen in Chapter Four, "Prayer: A Job Description."

When the disciples of Jesus struggled with how to pray, they turned to their master seeking guidance. The disciples were given the Lord's Prayer, which has a central place in our Christian spirituality. There is no better map to follow than our beloved *Pater Noster*. Chapter Five, then, is "Our Father: A Spiritual Map."

Along life's path there are many stumbling blocks and obstacles. We all have to deal with distractions, periods of dryness, lack of faith and trust, forgetfulness and that noonday devil that is known as acedia. Chapter Six, "Overcoming Prayer's Five Obstacles," reflects on how we might remove the impediments that hinder our union with God and with one another.

One of the tricky balancing acts in life is to devote sufficient time and energy to our private and public lives, to our personal and liturgical prayer. In a culture that stresses individualism we must not lose sight of our communal nature. At the same time, we cannot allow liturgy to replace personal time with the Lord. Chapter Seven examines "Prayer's Two Sides: Personal and Communal."

The concept of the individual's right to life, liberty and the pursuit of happiness has strong roots in our American tradition. Our Christian tradition informs us that happiness is so much more than material well-being; it is essentially a spiritual attitude grounded in a life of prayer and union with God. We focus on the relationship between prayer and happiness in Chapter Eight, "Eight Ways to Be Happy."

As Catholics, we are people of the word and the table, we are a eucharistic community. When we gather to celebrate the life, death and resurrection of the Lord we enter into the heart of our prayer life. Jesus empowers us to break open the word and Jesus comes to nourish us on our long journey. "Becoming a Eucharistic People," Chapter Nine, reflects on the Eucharist and its transformative power.

Prayer leads us ever more deeply into a life of discipleship and stewardship. Every relationship is sustained by serious conversation. This is obviously true about our being disciples of the Lord. More, prayer will call us to lives of stewardship, of tending well the gifts that God has given to us. In Chapter Ten, "The Heart of Discipleship," we discuss our vocation as stewards and disciples.

The bookends of Matthew's Gospel are the Beatitudes and the Last Judgment discourse. Here Jesus gives us his vision of blessedness and his standards for entering the Kingdom. Each of the eight Beatitudes draws us into prayer and meditation. Chapter Eleven will guide us in "Praying the Beatitudes."

A sage piece of advice: never travel alone. Our concluding chapter, "Nine Prayer Companions," offers reflections on mentors and companions for our journey of prayer. Our history is filled with individuals who experienced the Lord deeply in prayer and have articulated that encounter. Their insights and examples give us confidence and courage.

It is one thing to write about prayer; it is something else to pray. Let me end this Preface with a traditional prayer to Mary, the Mother of the Church, called the Memorare. Just as the disciples approached the Lord with their desire to pray, we too might ask Mary to intercede for us so that we might pray well. If we ask with confidence, our request will be granted:

Remember, O most gracious Virgin Mary, that never was it known that anyone who fled to thy protection, implored thy help or sought thy intercession, was left unaided. Inspired by this confidence, I fly unto thee, O Virgin of virgins, my mother: to thee I come, before thee I stand, sinful and sorrowful. O Mother of the Word Incarnate, despise not my petitions, but in thy mercy hear and answer me. Amen.

CHAPTER ONE

Prayer: 'Reversed Thunder'

My grandfather was a wise man. One piece of wisdom that remains with me was his statement that the three greatest blessings of his life were the gift of faith, the gift of friends and the gift of serious conversation.

Serious conversation! That puzzled me until the experiences of life taught me that dialogue is indeed a marvelous grace. Communication with friends leads to unity and joy; communication with God, which we call prayer, leads to union and peace.

The *Catechism of the Catholic Church* is concerned with what we believe (Part One), how we celebrate our beliefs (Part Two), how we live out our faith (Part Three) and about how we enter into serious conversation with God through our prayer (Part Four). In this collection of twelve essays I would like to explore with you some of the implications of our prayer life: what prayer is, the connection of prayer and daily life, the varieties of prayer and contemporary obstacles to this serious conversation, and the relationship between prayer and happiness.

President Harry S Truman memorized this prayer and used it through most of his life:

> O Almighty and Everlasting God, Creator of Heaven, Earth and the Universe: Help me to be, to think, to act what is right, because it is right; make me truthful, honest and honorable in all things; make me intellectually honest for the sake of right and honor and without thought of reward to me. Give me the ability to be charitable, forgiving and patient with my fellowmen—help me to understand their motives and their shortcomings— even as Thou understandst mine!

Prayer Is for Everyone

Who prays? Dads and moms as they strive to raise their children in a secular culture; teachers who know that without God's help they will have little influence on their students; doctors who beg God to guide them in their practice of healing the ill; farmers who understand that all life, all holiness comes from God; all people who are aware of their total dependency upon God and believe in God's providential love lift up their minds and hearts to God on a daily basis. The Gallup Organization, in fact, in 1994 reported that nine out of ten Americans say they pray.

But what is prayer? Prayer is about seeing God. So much of our lives is spent giving attention to the thousand and one activities of our daily life, some of which are necessary, some not. We are busy making a living, tending our gardens, planning for this or that celebration, doing the laundry, reading the newspaper or watching TV. Our vision may well fail to see God behind the gifts and graces of ordinary life. Our hearts may become cluttered and crowded by multiple relationships, by an abundance of possessions, by calendars that control our time. Suddenly (or not so suddenly) God may be pushed farther and farther from our consciousness. Secularism, an exclusive this-worldliness, can become a way of life. Prayer fades away.

According to the *Catechism* prayer is many things: "a surge of the heart [St. Therese of Lisieux, *Manuscrits autobiographiques* C25r]" (#2558); "raising of one's mind and heart to God [St. John Damascene, *De fide orth*. 3, 24: PG 94, 1089c]" (#2559); "the response of faith to the free promise of salvation and also a response of love to the thirst of the only Son of God [cf. Jn 7:37-39; 19:28; Is 12:3; 51:1; Zech 12:10; 13:1]" (#2561). Prayer is that basic communication between God and God's creatures that sustains and deepens a loving relationship.

One of my favorite images of prayer comes from the poet George Herbert (1593-1633) who understood prayer as "reversed thunder." Here is a portion of his poem:

> Prayer the Church's banquet, Angels' age,
> God's breath in man returning to his birth,
> The soul in paraphrase, heart in pilgrimage,
> The Christian plummet sounding heav'n and earth;
> Engine against th' Almighty...
> Reversed thunder....

God does communicate with us in a variety of ways: thunder (and lightning), Scripture, the sacraments, nature, personal relationships, the larger community, world events, our Tradition, the magisterium of the

Church, our intuitions, our dreams. And we respond to God's initiative in multiple ways: praise for divine glory, thanksgiving for small and great gifts, intercessions for needs, forgiveness for our sins and the sins of the world. Deep calling to deep, thunder to thunder, prayer is the mysterious dialogue between Creator and creature.

Several years ago I challenged a group of retreatants to memorize this four-line prayer written by the former Secretary General of the United Nations, Dag Hammarskjöld (1905-1961). In fact, jokingly I told them they would not be allowed to leave the retreat house until they memorized the prayer!

> Give me a pure heart—that I may see Thee,
> A humble heart—that I may hear Thee,
> A heart of love—that I may serve Thee,
> A heart of faith—that I may abide in Thee.
> (*Markings*, Alfred A. Knopf, Inc., 1966)

Praying is about seeing, hearing, serving; it's about abiding in God's loving and merciful presence. But certain conditions are essential to prayerfulness, to a way of life that is lived with an awareness of the mystery of God. In many ways the *Catechism* instructs us in the art of "reversed thunder" by emphasizing the need for purity, humility, love and faith. These four virtues are dispositions that enable us to live in God's presence and empower us to do God's will.

Before looking at the relationship between prayer and the virtues of purity, humility, love and faith, we do well to ponder a promise God makes to us through the prophet Ezekiel. It is a promise of a new heart, a new spirit. Our ability to pray is rooted in a gift that comes from God: "I will sprinkle clean water upon you, and you shall be clean from all your uncleannesses, and from all your idols I will cleanse you. A new heart I will give you, and a new spirit I will put within you; and I will remove from your body the heart of stone and give you a heart of flesh" (Ezekiel 36:25-27).

We rely not upon our own ability to pray as we ought. Rather, we have confidence that God will be true to the prophetic word and transform our lives by means of a new heart.

'Give Me a Pure Heart—That I May See Thee'

Several years ago I had an experience that helped me to see the connection between purity and seeing. I took my car to the car wash, paid my $7.95 and, as I drove out into the sunlight, I saw dirt left on the windshield that kept me from seeing. So too the soul is unable to see clearly when impurity dwells within our hearts.

Or take the case of wanting to spend the evening helping children with homework or doing some serious reading. If one indulges in too much food or wine at table, the mind and heart become sluggish. The body and mind must be purified in order to be truly present— whether to human experience or to God.

From all our idols and impurities God will cleanse us. Purity and seeing are linked together; so, too, purity and prayer. The *Catechism* puts it very concisely: "Purity of heart will enable us to see God: it enables us even now to see things according to God" (#2531).

Ronald Rolheiser, in his book *The Shattered Lantern:*

Rediscovering a Felt Presence of God (Crossroad, 1995), discusses a sense of purity and chastity that has somehow been lost in our society:

Chastity is normally defined as something to do with sex, namely, a certain innocence, purity, discipline, or even celibacy regarding sex. This, however, is too narrow. Chastity...has to do with the limits and appropriateness of all experiencing, the sexual included. To be chaste means to experience things, all things, respectfully and to drink them in only when we are ready for them. We break chastity when we experience anything irreverently or prematurely.

Experiencing things respectfully! A song from the 1960's (still heard in elevators, grocery stores and preschools!) is Simon and Garfunkel's "Feelin' Groovy," challenging us to "Slow down, you move too fast." If we don't slow down we miss the beauty of a sunset. We don't hear the cry of the poor, we fail to see the miracles that surround us, we are deaf to the whispers of God in our heart. Indeed, without a chaste heart, we miss life!

The prayer, "Give me a pure heart—that I may see Thee," simple on the surface, involves reverence and maturity. We pray for a reverence for the mystery of God who creates, redeems and sanctifies us. We pray for the maturity that calls us to a deeper awareness of our identity and destiny. We pray for a respect for all life that fosters holiness, the perfection of charity. Without a pure heart, reverence, maturity and respect are thwarted, if not destroyed.

'A Humble Heart—That I May Hear Thee'

Some years ago a popular singer sang, "Oh Lord, it's hard to be humble, when you're perfect in every way." The humor in this ditty needs no explanation. Unfortunately, there *are* people who see themselves from an exalted point of view, lacking all reality. The serious side in all this is that those who think they are perfect see no need for prayer.

"[H]*umility* is the foundation of prayer," teaches the *Catechism* (#2559). Humility roots us in the knowledge of truth about ourselves and about God. It provides a sense of proportion and reality, even to the point of fostering humor. How can we finite creatures "take in" the ocean of the mystery of God? How can we limited, earthly creatures understand the unlimited splendor of a Triune God? Humility allows us to smile.

Pride blocks hearing because ultimately pride is a lie. One of the most influential Christians of the twentieth century, Thomas Merton, struggled throughout his life to overcome pride and live in the land of humility. In prayer he would beg God to teach him humility. Merton honestly faced that fact that even in finding truth it was "half poisoned with deceit, and that the terrible thing about humility is that it is never fully successful."

One of the elementary principles of prayer is that we must bring the "real me" before the living and true God. This is why humility is the foundation of prayer. Without humble self-knowledge, we find ourselves in a position that God's word—whether affirming or confronting, consoling or challenging—has no authentic listener. To the proud, God's word does not fall on deaf ears; it falls into the abyss of the false self.

Our "reversed thunder," our humble prayer, is filled with wonder and awe. To believe that our God longs to speak to us and that God desires that we respond in love and adoration is overwhelming. Yet Jesus tells us how effective humility is when the tax collector, far to the back of the Temple, simply confesses his sins. That acknowledgement of sin and plea for mercy stirred the heart of God and forgiveness was given. The tax collector's almost inaudible thunder was heard by our great God while the Pharisee's loud boast simply re-echoed in his own arrogant heart. The Pharisee walked home humming a tune about how hard it is to be humble. The tax collector knew the mystery of God's peace and joy.

'A Heart of Love—That I May Serve Thee'

How do we know if our prayer is really authentic? That is a challenging question. Yet there is an answer in our Tradition: The authenticity of our prayer is proportionate to our love for our brothers and sisters. Our prayer is authentic if we fulfill God's command of love and service.

To be authentic, prayer must eventually spill over in compassionate care for our sisters and brothers. Jesus came to serve, not to be served. He called his disciples to a life of self-giving, even to the point of death. None of this is possible without the grace of love, that ability of self-donation, respect, reverence, responsibility. The new heart promised by God is one of charity which, when perfected, is holiness.

I recall once being moved by the insight of a catechist. She said that the way we witness to the gospel today is by making people feel that they are safe and that they are important. Love does not harm others. We provide an environment in which others do not have to fear. Love means that we help other people feel their worth, their dignity, their unique importance.

The *Catechism* reminds us that "In prayer, the faithful God's initiative of love always comes first; our own first step is always a response" (#2567). Prayer is love speaking to love, divine love engaging the human heart and receiving a response in return. Two concerns here: First, the inclination to doubt that we are lovable and, second, the need to transcend our imprisoning selfishness in order to become truly loving people.

Caught up in our narrow interests, parochial concerns, neurotic fears, we lack the freedom and generosity to respond appropriately to God and our fellow creatures. God's gift of a new heart of love empowers us to rise above our innate egotism and respond to the interests of God and the needs of our sisters and brothers. Workers in soup kitchens do this as they respectfully feed the hungry; moms and dads do this when they sacrifice for their children's education; teachers and counselors do this as they liberate minds and hearts from ignorance and fear.

Every baptized person is called to some form of ministry. Every baptized person is gifted with new life in Jesus, a life grounded in love and prayer: "Give me, Lord, a heart of love—that I may serve Thee."

'A Heart of Faith—That I May Abide in Thee'

In his autobiography, Alec Guinness speaks of coming to faith:

> The winter hills nourish my faith. There had been no emotional upheaval, no great insight, certainly no proper grasp of theological issues; just a sense of history and the fittingness of things. Something impossible to explain. Pere Teilhard de Chardin says, "The incommunicable part of us is the pasture of God." I must leave it at that. (*Blessings in Disguise*, Alfred A. Knopf, Inc., 1984)

Faith is that "pasture of God" wherein we abide with a God who is in us, above and below us, for us and always with us!

In the words of the *Catechism*, "One enters into prayer as one enters into liturgy: by the narrow gate of *faith*. Through the signs of his presence, it is the Face of the Lord that we seek and desire; it is his Word that we want to hear and keep" (#2656).

Faith involves a number of elements. One is courtesy, a gracious welcoming of God into our hearts. The Lord knocks at the door of our lives (see Revelation 3:20) and will abide with anyone who listens and shares in the divine life. Faith is a deep conviction that God truly desires to dwell with us in a loving covenant. By means of daily prayer we attune ourselves to God's presence.

A second element of faith is trust. When we are confident of God's saving help, when we quit relying completely on ourselves, then we allow God to transform us. Our hearts can sing "Amazing Grace" with vigor as we reflect prayerfully on how God—in the past and in the present—finds us who were lost, how God continues to help us see though once we were blind.

A third element of faith and prayer is our faithful assent to God's word. In prayer we focus on God's message of salvation, in particular, on the Beatitudes (Matthew 5) and the Last Judgment scene (Matthew 25). These are the bookends of our faith. We are not only to read these passages, not only to pray them from the heart, but to put them into practice. This is a living faith, one that moves from listening to doing.

While attending an ecumenical gathering in Philadelphia some years ago, I asked a participant what was the central belief of her faith. Without hesitation she responded: "I unreservedly and with abandon commit my life and destiny to Christ, promising to give him practical priority in all the affairs of my life. I will seek first the kingdom of God and his righteousness." I went home from that gathering desiring to have a faith as deep and as practical as hers.

A Concluding Prayer

Four days into the school year last autumn, first-grader Sam left home in the morning, his mother in bed with a serious cold. Sam was worried throughout the day and hurried home after school, anxious all the way, to find out happily that his mom was at the stove preparing dinner. Little Sam hugged his mom and shouted: "It worked, it worked!" "What worked?" his mother inquired. "I prayed all day that you would be all right and it worked, it worked!"

Prayer *does* work, prayer from the heart that is pure, humble, loving and faithful. Little Sam had a big heart, a prayerful heart, long before any formal religious instruction.

I told you earlier how I challenged my retreatants to memorize the prayer by Dag Hammarskjöld. Let me close with a challenge to my readers: Memorize Hammarskjöld's prayer and a second prayer, this one by Saint Richard of Chichester (1197-1253).

> Thanks be to Thee, my Lord Jesus Christ, for all the benefits which thou has given me, for all the pains and insults which thou hast borne for me, O most merciful friend, redeemer and brother. May I see Thee more clearly, love Thee more dearly and follow Thee more nearly.

I promise you that if you pray these two prayers from the heart on a daily basis, your life will take on a depth and quality you never dreamt of.

Growing in Faith

- *What style of prayer is most attractive to you?*

- *Do you think God communicates with people? How?*

- *Why do we say that prayer starts with God?*

- *Has pride ever blocked your prayer? How?*

Prayer in Practice

Copy these prayers and fasten them to your bathroom mirror or refrigerator:

Give me a pure heart—that I may see Thee,
A humble heart—that I may hear Thee,
A heart of love—that I may serve Thee,
A heart of faith—that I may abide in Thee.
                    —*Dag Hammarskjöld*

Thanks be to Thee, my Lord Jesus Christ, for all the benefits which thou has given me, for all the pains and insults which thou hast borne for me, O most merciful friend, redeemer and brother. May I see Thee more clearly, love Thee more dearly and follow Thee more nearly.
                    —*Saint Richard of Chichester*

CHAPTER TWO

Five Principles of Prayer

Gabriel the archangel and the Virgin Mary, in stained glass, illumine the Church of the Annunciation in Altamonte Springs, Florida. Etched in glass is Gabriel's greeting to Mary: "The Lord is with you," and, in brilliant color, her response to the invitation to become Jesus' mother: "Be it done unto me according to your word." Above the angel and the virgin shines the cross.

That window tells in a single picture the essence of our Christian life and the meaning of prayer. When all is said and done, prayer always comes back to listening and responding. We are challenged to listen to God's word and to respond affirmatively.

To gaze reverently upon a mystery of faith is itself a prayer. But it is also important to *say* what we see, to wrap words, however inadequately, around the mystery so that we can share our experience of insight and affection with others. In sharing our faith we grow; in finding words to speak about the Word, we discover truth.

The *Catechism* provides us with words and insights and wisdom. This carefully crafted text offers many principles of prayer, general statements and guidelines that help us to understand prayer and put that understanding into practice. These principles are not abstractions but more like stained-glass windows, inviting a reverent glance, stirring the heart with affection, prodding the will to a greater commitment to God's will. The five principles we will examine are: (1) God takes the initiative in the dance of prayer; (2) prayer is a vital necessity; (3) hearken and do not harden; (4) prayer is both enlightening and empowering; (5) Christian prayer is trinitarian.

God Takes the Initiative

"In prayer, the faithful God's initiative of love always comes first; our own first step is always a response" (#2567).

The phone rings. Someone has taken the initiative to call. You pick up the receiver and the conversation begins. Words are spoken and responses are made. Some phone calls are more important than others: "Will you go to the prom with me?" "Are you willing to serve on the social justice committee?" "Will you be willing to take in a foreign exchange student?" Life is never the same after such calls.

The Virgin Mary received a life-changing call via the archangel Gabriel. God's initiative in her life was sudden, unexpected, transformative. In this great moment of prayer, all history hung in balance. Would Mary say yes or no to God's unique plan to come among us in human form? Mary gave her mystical yes even though she experienced fear and did not know exactly how this plan was to be fulfilled. Mary acted in faith. The Annunciation story is a superb example of how God leads us in the dance we call prayer.

How does God break into our lives, initiating a relationship that changes the color of our days? Our God is ingenious. Sometimes God comes through the tenderness of a parent, the challenge of a teacher, the pain of a broken relationship. At other times, we experience divine presence in an autumn moon, the taste of pumpkin pie, the song of the lark. Each of these moments is an opportunity for grace. So we give thanks for the health of a newborn, rejoice in the gift of a new friend, praise the Lord for the marvelous mystery of the Eucharist, beg forgiveness for the hurts that diminish our humanity. Mary responded courageously to God's initiative in her life.

The *Catechism* reminds us: "The wonder of prayer is revealed beside the well where we come seeking water: there, Christ comes to meet every human being. It is he who first seeks us and asks us for a drink.... Whether we realize it or not, prayer is the encounter of God's thirst with ours. God thirsts that we may thirst for him [cf. St. Augustine, *De diversis quaestionibus octosinta tribus* 64, 4: PL 40, 56]" (#2560).

Every morning we are invited to the well to receive God's word for the day. We might hear words like "Carry one another's burdens" or "Stop by and see Sam at the nursing home" or "Take some time off" (a message I particularly like to hear!).

Every evening we return to give an accounting of our stewardship. "Sorry, Lord, got caught up in my own agenda and never did get to the nursing home." Or, "I did three random acts of kindness today and made some people feel real good." Or, "Lord, tomorrow I really do intend to listen to your gentle proddings."

Prayer is a love relationship, a covenant of deep mutuality. It is a dance, but one in which we know who has the lead (at least, theoretically). It is a dance that invites a gracious following. Like Mary, we experience joy and peace when we, too, give a full and unconditional affirmative response.

Prayer Is a Vital Necessity

Some things in life are optional: pierced ears, a color TV, a video game, a soft drink. It is possible to live without them. Other things are vital, absolutely necessary for our humanity. Just to mention a few: eating and breathing—matters of life or death; reading and writing—if mature education is to happen; grace and prayer—vital elements in our spiritual lives. If these ingredients are not present, death occurs.

In the words of the *Catechism*, "*Prayer is a vital necessity.* Proof from the contrary is no less convincing: if we do not allow the Spirit to lead us, we fall back into the slavery of sin [cf. Gal 5:16-25]. How can the Holy Spirit be our life if our heart is far from him?" (#2744).

No prayer, we die spiritually. No communication, relationships diminish, vanish. No discipline, health deteriorates and is lost.

In the Annunciation story, Mary knew what was necessary if she was to be true to herself and to her God: obedience. She must listen to God's invitation and then respond with all her heart and soul. Her yes was necessary if she was to be true to her unique calling.

Some people say no to God's invitations. In James

Joyce's novel, *A Portrait of the Artist as a Young Man*, young Stephen Daedelus proclaims a bold "I will not serve" when presented with a harsh, judgmental God. In the Book of Genesis, Cain refused to accept his role in life and killed his brother.

One of the major confusions in our culture regards needs and wants. Birds "know" that they need air, not a fancy birdhouse with 18 rooms; fish "know" that they need water, not an Olympic-size swimming pool with a 20-foot diving board. When *wants* become *needs* we cross over the border into the land of idolatry. When true needs go unmet, we commit spiritual suicide.

Prayer is not a luxury. It is more than a friendly invitation. Prayer is an imperative, a demand, a vital necessity. But our God never imposes a command without giving the necessary resources. Thus we are given the Holy Spirit who prays within us. One of the fundamental teachings of the Church is that we are temples of the Holy Spirit.

Last year I read the autobiography of the great Hindu leader Mohandas K. Gandhi. He was convinced that the Western world is living with the great illusion that we are autonomous. By this he meant that we live with a false self-reliance, unaware that we are connected to our environment, to others, to God, in deep and meaningful ways. This insight struck me deeply. God in fact dwells with us and it is the presence of God's Spirit that empowers us to grow in responsibility and love.

Hearken and Do Not Harden

"We learn to pray at certain moments by hearing the

Word of the Lord and sharing in his Paschal mystery, but his Spirit is offered us at all times, in the events of *each day*, to make prayer spring up from us. Jesus' teaching about praying to our Father is in the same vein as his teaching about providence [cf. Mt 6:11, 34]: time is in the Father's hands; it is in the present that we encounter him, not yesterday nor tomorrow, but today: 'O that *today* you would hearken to his voice! Harden not your hearts' [Psalm 95:7-8]" (#2659).

This principle of prayer has two dimensions—listening to God's voice and not closing our hearts. First, God's voice can be drowned out by the many voices that fill our air waves. Politicians tell us to vote this or that way; TV commercials tell us what to eat, drink and buy; our peers tell us what to wear and how to act. The Church offers moral guidance. God speaks softly.

In our pluralistic society, then, how do we hearken to God's voice, today, here and now? If prayer is an authentic listening, where can we go? Here are four channels that have been major resources for me:

Turn to the Bible. God speaks to us in the Scriptures, revealing the mysteries of creation, redemption, our sanctification. God says that creation is good, that we need to be redeemed from sin, that the Spirit is given for holiness. God says that we are to love one another as he loves us, that we are to forgive seven times seventy times, that we are not to judge and condemn. We must hearken to this voice in a world of contrary voices.

Turn to the teaching of the Church to hear God's voice. We have been blessed in a special way with the marvelous documents of Vatican II, with challenging social encyclicals, with letters on peace and justice and evangelization. God speaks to us through the magisterium and our two-thousand-year Tradition.

Be attentive to everyday experience. God speaks in a child's smile, a verse from a good poem, in the cry of the poor, in the invitation to tithe, in the challenge to end a relationship that is destructive. If we are attentive to the wonder of breakfast cereal, a teenager's silent request for help, ecological consciousness-raising—if we are attentive, we will hear God calling us.

Listen to God speaking in our hearts. We have been given a conscience, that strange but real inner voice, that registers right and wrong. Though that faculty might grow lax or hardened, it still has the capacity to be an instrument of divine intervention. By hearkening to our conscience and the intuitions of the soul, we might hear today the voice of the Spirit.

Not only must we hearken; we must not harden our hearts. Prayer is a matter of the heart, a matter of love. If the heart is stony, the seeds of God's word will not find receptive soil. We must beg God for a heart of hospitality.

On a retreat with teenagers I asked what a heart of hospitality might look like. The teens drew a large heart on the blackboard and labeled sections of the heart: Open Space, Warm Welcome, Attentive Presence and Generous Service. Being hospitable, they explained, we create a space for others to enter, for God to come into our homes. We take warm delight in the presence of others, and pay close attention to them. I observed that when Mary sat at the feet of Jesus she offered hospitality at a deeper level than Martha did. Being *with* our guest, God's Word, is one of the deepest forms of prayer. Finally, my young friends observed that when someone comes to visit us, we must be ready and willing to respond to their authentic needs, even to the point of sacrifice. What insight!

Too often our hearts are hardened, lacking hospitality. We are too busy with our own agenda. We are inattentive to the experiences around us because of hurriedness or apathy. We are unwilling to sacrifice our precious and limited time for the needs of others.

Prayer is about hearkening and receptivity. But again, this is not simply our own work. The Spirit will give us a new heart and put a new spirit within us so that today we might hear and do God's word.

Prayer Enlightens and Empowers

After the children are raised, what's next? My job holds no more challenge, should I move on? An injustice has come to light, what should be done? Something stirs within me to reach out to the poor, what does this mean? "By prayer we can discern 'what is the will of God' and obtain the endurance to do it [Rom 12:2; cf. Eph 5:17; cf. Heb 10:36]" (#2826).

C.S. Lewis maintained that in the end there are only two types of people: those who do God's will and those who do their own. Prayer helps us to discern God's will in our life. We ponder the movements in the soul (nudges, whispers, proddings) to see whether or not they come from God or some other source. In our private prayer we enter into silence and solitude seeking the enlightenment of the Spirit. In public prayer, worship, we join our brothers and sisters in reflecting upon God's words and ways. We ask for the courage and power to do what is asked of us in our unique circumstances.

In the movie *The Mission*, about eighteenth-century Jesuits in South America, the priests had to make a decision: to pick up weapons to defend the people or to take a pacifist stance, refusing to use violence to confront violence. One priest picked up the sword and fought, another carried a monstrance with the Blessed Sacrament through the village. Both priests prayed. Both sought enlightenment and empowerment. Both made decisions that they would have to live with for the rest of their lives.

We, too, need to pray to decide whether or not to ground a teenager for breaking a rule, to leave or stay with a job when being asked to do something that is wrong, to confess or remain silent about one's sins. Decisions have to be made and responsibility assumed. Despite lacking full knowledge, we live on a planet where risk is always part of the human condition. But if we pray, we can be assured of God's gracious assistance.

A favorite passage of mine comes from Robert Coles's *The Spiritual Life of Children* (Houghton Mifflin Company, 1990), in which nine-year-old Mary tells of her desire: "I don't want to waste my time here on this earth. When you're put here, it is for a reason. The Lord wants you to do something. If you don't know what, then you've got to try hard to find out what. It may take time. You may make mistakes. But if you pray, He'll lead you to your direction. He won't hand you a piece of paper with a map on it, no sir. He'll whisper something, and at first you may not even hear but if you have trust in Him and you keep turning to Him, it will be all right."

Prayer moves beyond enlightenment into the doing. We must act on our own. Little Mary asked for a direction so as not to waste her life. As she grew up I tend to think that she constantly prayed to God to give her the energy to act on the direction given. Authentic prayer can be measured by the life lived.

Christian Prayer Is Trinitarian

Christian prayer is a covenant relationship between God and humanity. Says the *Catechism*: "It is the action of God and of man, springing forth from both the Holy Spirit and ourselves, wholly directed to the Father, in union with the human will of the Son of God made man" (#2564).

Two fundamental forms express the dialogue between God and humanity: "[O]ur prayer *ascends* in the Holy Spirit through Christ to the Father—we bless him for having blessed us [cf. Eph 1:3-14; 2 Cor 1:3-7; 1 Pt 1:3-9]; it implores the grace of the Holy Spirit that *descends* through Christ from the Father—he blesses us" (#2627).

In the Annunciation stained-glass window in Florida, with Mary, the angel and the cross, there is something that cannot be seen but is present—the mystery of the Trinity. In faith we know that God the Father is there, sending the angel; Jesus is there in the moment of the Incarnation; the Holy Spirit is present in overshadowing Mary and all of history.

Christian prayer is trinitarian. Every time we gather at Mass we begin by making the Sign of the Cross, which reminds us who we are. When we sign ourselves consciously and reverently, we are a prayerful people. That powerful symbol tells us whose we are and marks us as God's people.

It wasn't until seventh grade that I understood the difference between a principle and the principal. It wasn't until several years after high school that I realized that unless we had a principled principal our school was going nowhere.

So too on our spiritual journey. Christians who have principles know to some degree what direction to take, what paths to avoid. In and of themselves principles do not save but they do lead closer to the Savior. Without these markings we get lost in the forest.

My fifth principle requires your meditation more than my explanation: "Love is the source of prayer" (#2658).

Growing in Faith

- *Is prayer a luxury or necessity in your life?*

- *Why is it difficult to hear God's voice in our world?*

- *What are three of your favorite passages from Scripture, passages in which God speaks to your heart?*

- *Is "dancing" a good analogy for prayer? Why or why not?*

Prayer in Practice

The poet Jessica Powers sings of her relationship to a Triune God. This prayer-poem is a magnificent summary of our fifth, trinitarian principle of prayer:

Doxology

God fills my being to the brim
with floods of His immensity.
I drown within a drop of Him
whose sea-bed is infinity.

The Father's will is everywhere
for chart and chance His precept keep.
There are no beaches to His care
nor cliffs to pluck from His deep.

The Son is never far away from me
for presence is what love compels.
Divinely and incarnately
He draws me where His mercy dwells.

And lo, myself am the abode
of Love, the third of the Triune,
the primal surge and sweep of God
and my eternal claimant soon!

Praise to the Father and the Son
and to the Spirit! May I be,
O Water, Wave and Tide in One,
thine animate doxology.

CHAPTER THREE

Seven Habits of Prayerful People

How easily the golfing pro drives a ball 280 yards! How gracefully the Olympic skater glides across the ice! How effortlessly the master teacher communicates even difficult concepts! But we are not fooled. We know that behind the apparent ease, grace and spontaneity are years of discipline and training—the habits that have shaped the golfer, ice skater, teacher into a pro.

Dr. M. Scott Peck's best-seller *The Road Less Traveled* (Simon and Schuster, Inc., 1978) emphasizes discipline grounded in habits. A habit is a disposition to perform certain actions according to a pattern. Grateful people say "thank you" for even a small gift. Courteous individuals are respectful of others in word and manner. Prayerful people turn their minds and hearts to God on a regular basis.

Habits come in two flavors. Positive habits are called virtues because they give life and nurture relationships. But poisonous habits, vices, such as lying, cheating and insensitivity, are death-dealing to the self and to the common good.

Just as healthy intellectual habits help us learn and

habits of thrift help our finances, so our spiritual routines enable us to accomplish our goals: union with God and unity with one another. Raising our minds and hearts to God is essential for achieving our destiny. Prayerful people develop good habits, solid virtues, that help keep them attuned and responsive to God's call in the events of daily life.

Reading through Part Four of the *Catechism* I see that a number of habits emerge. Here are seven that will further our intimacy with God and lead to building God's reign.

1. Walk With God

Adam and Eve walked with God in the Garden. *Genesis* also shows Enoch and Noah finding God in the realities of creation, "walking with God" with hearts "upright and undivided." In the words of the *Catechism*, "This kind of prayer is lived by many righteous people in all religions" (#2569).

In shopping malls, people are in the habit of walking around and around for exercise, talking about common interests. Wise spouses regularly set aside time for sharing their lives, maybe while taking a walk.

Prayerful people walk with God every day. This "walking" can be done kneeling beside your bed to thank God for a restful sleep or to ask the Lord to guide your day. This "walking" might take place while driving to work or take the form of singing in the shower at the joy of being alive. Feeding the birds might serve as a reminder of God's loving providence.

Walking with God embraces a sense of

companionship. The two disciples on the road to Emmaus in Luke's Gospel had lost their hope, that habit of awareness that sustains a trustful reliance on God's help. Suddenly the disguised, risen Lord walks with them and explains the Scriptures. The hearts of the disciples once again are ablaze with a new fire. Walking with God is transformative. (You'll find the story in Luke 24:13-32.)

Walking with God is a faith experience. The great Jewish writer Abraham Heschel reflects: "The issue of prayer is not prayer; the issue of prayer is God. One cannot pray unless he has faith in his own ability to accost the infinite, merciful, eternal God" (*Man's Quest for God*, Charles Scribner's Sons, 1954). Faith is that profound conviction that God is with us and for us.

From a different angle, it is not so much our walking with God as it is God walking with us in the cool of the evening, in the heat of the noonday sun, in the early hours of dawn. The habit of faith connects us to the Origin and Sustainer of all life. This habit, both a gift and a task, keeps us conscious of God's abiding love and fidelity.

2. Reverence Beginnings and Endings

A year ago I had the opportunity of traveling to and from Chicago with a friend of mine, now in his mid-seventies. As we began the two-hundred-mile journey, my friend made the Sign of the Cross and prayed the Hail Mary. Upon our arrival in the Windy City he did the same.

He told me that every single time he rode with his

parents they went through this same ritual. The family began and ended trips with a prayer. They began and ended their meals with a prayer. It was as natural as breathing and it was not done carelessly. The words came from the heart and were uttered with conviction.

Prayerful people have the habit of reverence, especially as they begin and end each experience. Of course, that same reverence will permeate the entire happening. Saint Catherine of Siena, a doctor of the Church, speaks about the soul who lives with reverent prayerfulness: "She holds all things in reverence, the left hand as well as the right, trouble as well as consolation, hunger and thirst as well as eating and drinking, cold and heat and nakedness as well as clothing, life as well as death, honor as well as disgrace, distress as well as comfort" (*The Dialogue*, Paulist Press, 1980).

Not all events have equal weight. Just a second or two may suffice in starting and stopping lesser moments of life. But major decisions, like selecting a partner for life, pondering a change of employment, discerning one's vocation, might demand many hours and even days of prayer and reflection.

It comes down to taking seriously our lives as a covenant relationship with God. We do not live or act alone. God is with us every step of the way. Our challenge is to be mindful of that divine presence and to act in accord with God's will. In the *Catechism* we read: "'No one can say "Jesus is Lord" except by the Holy Spirit' [1 Cor 12:3].... That is why the Church invites us to call upon the Holy Spirit every day, especially at the beginning and the end of every important action" (#2670).

3. Rely on God's Promises

People getting married promise each other their love and fidelity. In signing contracts, employers and employees commit themselves to mutual obligations. A mother drops off the kids for a movie and promises to be back in two hours. Promise-making and promise-keeping hold families and society together. Once trust has been broken, once promises are not kept, things fall apart.

Our God is a promise-maker and prayer puts us in contact with what God has vowed to do. And what are some of God's promises? One is that God will be with us always. It is a promise of presence and abiding concern.

Another is God's promise to give us a new heart (see Ezekiel 36:25-29). Perhaps we do not feel a need for a new heart and a new spirit but, honestly, there is a hardness and a meanness within each of our lives that needs a new spirit. What is called for is not bypass surgery but a heart transplant.

A third promise is the gift of divine life. God's presence is powerful, a new heart and spirit is transformative, but God's gift is a promise of infinite Love. Daily prayer exposes us to the mystery of God's self-offer. This is the life of grace, this is the incredible mystery of God's supreme commitment to the world.

In a powerful scene from Thornton Wilder's *The Skin of Our Teeth*, a wife comments to her husband on the motive of marriage: "I didn't marry you because you were perfect. I didn't even marry you because I loved you. I married you because you gave me a promise."

She takes off her ring and looks at it. "That promise made up for your faults. And the promise I gave you made up for mine. Two imperfect people got married and it was the promise that made the marriage."

God's marriage to us, God's covenant, is the promise that comes to us in daily prayer. It calls us to respond with fidelity to a God who is worthy of our total reliance.

4. Pray Constantly

My brother once owned an old Ford Ferguson tractor which eventually became quite temperamental. One day it would start, the next day it would refuse.

Our prayer life has its ups and downs. When the weather is fair, when we are healthy, and especially when things are going our way, prayer can be fairly easy and constant. But come the storms of fate or illness or defeat, we often find it hard to fall to our knees. We fail to heed the admonition at the beginning of the preface of the Mass that says: "It is right and just that we always and everywhere give thanks to the Lord."

Can we pray constantly, given the fact that we live in a world of many distractions? We are even advised by tradition and wisdom figures to give full attention to the here-and-now. Is it possible and realistic to pray always?

Authentic friends love one another constantly. Even though they may be separated by geography or apart for months on end, their love not only does not diminish but grows. Below our daily involvements there are other levels of consciousness and awareness. In the midst of baking bread, one's heart can be attuned to God's abiding life; during the course of a lecture, the Spirit can be invoked; while plowing a field, the farmer might well be aware of Christ's presence in the beauty of the autumn.

This habit of praying constantly is like our breathing or the beating of the heart. For the heart to stop or the breath to cease means death. When we fail to pray our soul begins to wither and die. Constant prayer keeps us spiritually sound and healthy.

Thus we are encouraged by the *Catechism*: "'Pray constantly...always and for everything giving thanks in the name of our Lord Jesus Christ to God the Father' [1 Thes 5:17; Eph 5:20].... This tireless fervor can come only from love. Against our dullness and laziness, the battle of prayer is that of humble, trusting, and persevering *love*. This love opens our hearts to three enlightening and life-giving facts of faith about prayer" (#2742). These three are: It is always possible to pray; prayer is a vital necessity; and prayer and Christian life are inseparable.

5. Act Truthfully

One aspect of prayer is conversation. God speaks to us through Scripture, nature, the teaching of the Church; we speak to God in words of adoration, thanksgiving, petition. But prayer has another level that takes us from the realm of verbal exchange to the incarnating of those words into actions. Theologians call this *orthopraxis*, the doing of the word or prayer in our daily life. Others call it putting your money where your mouth is, or "walking your talk."

Jesus tells us that in the end the sheep and goats will be separated, not by how deeply they believed, not by the depth of affection in the heart, but by their treatment of fellow human beings. The sheep enter the Kingdom because they fed the hungry and gave drink to the thirsty. The goats are embraced by darkness because they failed to visit prisons and take in the stranger.

The habit of acting truthfully is simple and clear: Truth is put into action. That assumes we can grasp the truth (or that the Truth can grasp us) and second, that we have sufficient freedom to act on it.

We need here the virtue of prudence, the habit of making right decisions. Put simply, prudence is seeing, judging and acting. But there can be hitches. We don't always see well, either the truth of our own being or the complex truths of our world. Sometimes we hesitate because all the facts are not in. This can lead to a life of procrastination (the art of catching up with yesterday!). Then again, we may know the truth and make correct judgments, but not have the energy, courage or conviction to put the truth into practice.

Some advice from the *Catechism*: "To meditate on what we read helps us to make it our own by confronting it with ourselves. Here, another book is opened: the book of life. We pass from thoughts to reality. To the extent that we are humble and faithful, we discover in meditation the movements that stir the heart and we are able to discern them. It is a question of acting truthfully in order to come into the light: 'Lord, what do you want me to do?'" (#2706).

This fifth habit relies upon a threefold grace: prudence, humility and faithfulness.

6. Persevere

Our century has been turbulent. The scars of world wars, the brutality of the Holocaust, the ethnic cleansings, the alienation consequent upon oppression, all provide sufficient evidence for discouragement, if not despair. It is not surprising that some people quit on life, giving up the ghost before the ghost of death comes.

I heard a powerful story of a husband and wife who were traveling in the north of Belgium. They came across a notice that in the afternoon a concert was to be given in a small church in the local village. They went with few expectations. But to their surprise, a 93-year-old pianist, blind and infirm, came out and played selections from Mozart for two hours, holding the small audience of some fifty people in awe.

This comment was made: "For over eighty years, cutting across an age marked by wars and devastation, this woman shared with the world the beauty of classical music. Despite the darkness and violence, she persevered in bringing beauty to the world. She refused to quit."

Our times are not hospitable to stick-to-itiveness! When things get tough in relationships, we split. When a new course of studies becomes difficult, we withdraw. When God is silent, we stop praying. If we don't get our way immediately, we're out of here!

Another alternative from the *Catechism*:

Finally, our battle has to confront what we experience as *failure in prayer*: discouragement during periods of dryness; sadness that, because we have "great possessions" [cf. Mk 10:22], we have not given all to the Lord; disappointment over not being heard according to our own will; wounded pride, stiffened by the indignity that is ours as sinners; our resistance to the idea that prayer is a free and unmerited gift; and so forth. The conclusion is always the same: what good does it do to pray? To overcome these obstacles, we must battle to gain humility, trust, and perseverance. (#2728)

7. Keep Watch

The ancient Romans used an expression: "*Age hoc!*" It was a cry for people to pay attention, to be alert, to keep vigilance. This advice is valuable while difficult to live. To be present to the mystery of life is an art mastered by few.

The habit of attentiveness confronts our addictions, those areas of our life where we are not free. Dr. Gerald May writes: "Addiction and its associated mind tricks inevitably kidnap and distort our attention, profoundly hindering our capacity for love. Attention and love are intimate partners; for love to be actualized, attention must be free" (*Addiction and Grace*, HarperSanFrancisco, 1988).

When the Gospels so often speak about blindness and deafness, we realize that all of us suffer from these maladies. We do not see and hear because we are not free. We are not attentive to God's invasions of grace because our consciousness is held captive by people, things or events that have become obsessions.

The habit of watchfulness, vigilance and

attentiveness demands continual exercise. It also demands the grace of God. It is here that human intention and divine life come together. God's Spirit empowers us to be attentive; that same Spirit enables us to carry the attentiveness into practice.

This passage from the *Catechism* deserves careful study and prayer:

> In Jesus "the Kingdom of God is at hand" [Mk 1:15]. He calls his hearers to conversion and faith, but also to *watchfulness*. In prayer the disciple keeps watch, attentive to Him Who Is and Him Who Comes, in memory of his first coming in the lowliness of the flesh, and in the hope of his second coming in glory [cf. Mk 13; Lk 21:34-36]. In communion with their Master, the disciples' prayer is a battle; only by keeping watch in prayer can one avoid falling into temptation. (#2612)

The character of our personal life and that of our society is conditioned to a large extent by the formation of habits. The quality of our spiritual life is shaped by the same reality. Habits of the soul will ultimately determine our destiny.

Phyllis McGinley's *Saint-Watching* (Doubleday, 1974) has this line: "The habit of kindness thrives on practice. Charity is an infection hard to shake off." So, too, prayer is a habit that thrives on practice and will lead us into the infectious land of love.

Growing in Faith

- *What helps you to be aware of God's loving presence?*

- *What ways of praying have been successful in your life?*

- *How is it possible to "pray constantly"?*

- *Name a promise of God that touches you.*

Prayer in Practice

Seven Habits of Prayerful People

- *Walk with God.*

- *Reverence beginnings and endings.*

- *Rely on God's promises.*

- *Pray constantly.*

- *Act truthfully.*

- *Persevere.*

- *Keep watch.*

CHAPTER FOUR

Prayer: A Job Description

A job description tells us what we can expect to do. Prayer's job description tells us what we can count on prayer doing for us.

The *Catechism* gives us such a job description of prayer and outlines its wondrous benefits. Prayer: (1) reveals to us the mystery of God (#2558); (2) restores us to God's image (#2572, 2713); (3) keeps the memory of Jesus alive in our minds and hearts (#2625); (4) draws everything into Christ's love (#2658, 2572); (5) helps us to internalize and assimilate the Mass and Sacraments, leading us to union with God (#2655).

Prayer Reveals God's Mystery

People who own the new miniature TV satellite dishes have access to a variety of new worlds. Prayer is like a dish that gives us access to divine transmissions. We can pick up messages from a God who is filled with wisdom, compassion, forgiveness and love. But we have to position ourselves to receive the signal.

Prayer is the disposition of heart and the openness of mind to recognize and desire God's revelations. Prayer's task is to respond to God's self-disclosure. For

Moses, God's disclosure was the burning bush; for a new mom, God speaks through the miracle of a healthy baby; for the farmer, an abundant harvest; for the anxious immigrant, a welcoming community; for the worker, through the dignity of work.

God unveils divine wonders in ways which we humans are often too busy to see. Many don't notice that "earth's crammed with heaven" (Elizabeth Barrett Browning), or that "the world is charged with the grandeur of God" (Gerard Manley Hopkins).

God's revelation often comes unexpectedly and can turn our world upside-down. Some revelations are disturbing and show our dark side, our greed and selfishness. Other revelations are freeing and help us know that we are loved and the object of God's concern.

When we humbly turn our minds and hearts to God, God invites us into a life-giving relationship that is new and unending. God is the one from whom all life flows, the one who heals and restores our brokenness, the one who empowers us to share with others the love and forgiveness we have received. For Christians, God is powerfully revealed in the two great mysteries of the Trinity and the Incarnation. God is most perfectly revealed in Jesus.

Years ago a retreat director compared God to a principal of a school. The principal had three voices. In the opening assembly the principal spoke with a loud and authoritative voice that commanded respect. The principal used a second voice in speaking in the privacy of his office with parents of a troubled student, a voice filled with understanding and mercy. The principal had a third, silent and compassionate voice as he attended the wake of a student killed in a car accident. One principal, three voices. One God, three ways of addressing creation: the Holy Trinity.

To receive God's revelation, two conditions are important. First, we must take time for prayer. Friends deepen their knowledge of one another when they spend time in serious conversation. We have to make a value decision as to the importance of prayer in our life.

Second, we must give up our preconceived and erroneous ideas of God. Thinking of God as a harsh judge, as distant as a galaxy or disinterested in messy human problems, hinders us from accepting what God wants to communicate to us.

A woman on a much-needed retreat sought to know more about God and herself. She prayed, "Who are you and who am I?" For three days she prayed this refrain over a hundred times but no answer came. As she was leaving the retreat grounds she tried a last time: "Who are you and who am I?" An answer came, a revelation: "I am God and you are not!"

In that answer lies the meaning of prayer. God is our loving, creating, sanctifying God—we are creatures who are not lords of this world or of our own lives. God is our Maker, our Sustainer and our End.

Prayer Restores Us to God's Image

The expression "spitting image" refers to the likeness of a daughter to her mother, a son to his father. The resemblance is so forceful that, were it not for the fact of age, gray hair and wrinkles, it might be difficult to tell the parent from the child.

We are called to be the "spitting image" of God, a God who is filled with compassion, kindness, patience and love. Obviously, something has gone wrong. The image of God in us has been tarnished, sometimes nearly obliterated. A restoration is needed and not just an external refurbishing. A profound transformation is in order so that we might once again find our true face and authentic voice. Prayer helps that transformation.

High school biology students learn about osmosis, the transfer of one substance into another organism through the porous cell walls. In non-scientific terms, we become what we get next to.

Prayer puts us "next to" God, next to divine truth, beauty and goodness. The proximity, when sustained and done with great commitment, works a radical change. God's truth speaks to our mind and new meanings are found. God's beauty washes over our soul, cleansing us of ugly dispositions and mean-spiritedness. God's goodness sets before us a model of holiness, the perfection of charity.

The opposite is also true. If we spend significant time before images of consumerism, next to falsity and ugliness, close to evil and cruelty, our inner life becomes stained and polluted; thus the challenge to be highly selective in our choice of entertainment and friends.

Jesus then becomes the portrait and model of discipleship. In prayer we draw near to the compassionate Jesus at Cana, the challenging Jesus in Jericho, the forgiving Jesus on the cross at Calvary. Prayer brings us into the presence of Jesus, within range of his outstretched arms. The redemptive Spirit of Jesus, encountered in prayer, leads to salvation.

Perhaps the greatest need for restoration in our life lies in the area of truth. Pope John Paul II has consistently urged upon the Church and the world the need to align our use of freedom with the truth of things. On his visit to our country in October, 1995, he cried out: "Every generation of Americans needs to know that freedom consists not in doing what we like but in having the right to do what we ought." And what ought we to do? The truth! And where can we discover the truth? In prayer!

Prayer discloses to us the truth of God's love and mercy, the truth of the dignity of every single person, the truth of our individual and collective sin, the truth of the Holy Spirit bending over our bent world. We need again to become scriptural people, familiar with the word of God. We need again to recover a sense of the common good and our call to universal solidarity. We need again to go down to the potter's shed and be reshaped and restored into God's image (see Jeremiah 18).

In Baptism we began a unique participation in God's life, sealed as we were with sacred oil. Again in Confirmation we were signed to image Christ as witness of faith. Prayer keeps reminding us of who (whose) we are—baptized and confirmed into the Paschal Mystery.

Not to pray leads to forgetfulness. Forgetfulness means that we will soon lose our sense of identity, our imaging of God. When we don't pray we are swimming in dangerous water.

Prayer Remembers Jesus

Alzheimer's is one of the dreaded diseases of life. The mind gradually loses its power to recall names and dates. As the illness progresses, the day comes when one cannot identify family members, cannot even remember one's own identity. On the spiritual level there is a similar kind of Alzheimer's. We forget about the mystery of God. We fail to live in the divine presence. We no longer know who Jesus is and thereby lose our sense of discipleship.

Prayer, that special time and space devoted to being with God, is a primary means of keeping the memory of Jesus alive. In a real sense, prayer is a school. Here we are instructed, formed and transformed through insight and experience.

One year I attended a Christmas program put on by the children in an Amish elementary school. The fifty-nine students sang songs, performed sketches, exchanged gifts for two hours. What I observed was really a prayer time. During those two hours the students and the observers were exposed to the memory of Jesus: the words of "Silent Night" (in German, of course), the sketches about the Magi following the star, the theme of light shining in our darkness.

What happens when we no longer sing our Christian songs, do our Christian rituals, share our bread together? Gradually the community falls apart and we follow other visions and values. We become illiterate in our understanding and non-responsive to the gospel imperative of love and forgiveness.

The problem is not that the knowledge of Jesus is

gone; our libraries are filled with Bibles, theological studies, Church documents. But without rituals, the memory of Jesus is stored and packed away. We must unpack the Good News once again, each age for itself, each person for himself or herself. Prayer is one way the memory of Jesus is kept alive and retains its power to shape our character, our culture and our society.

God gives us memory, too, so that when someone does us wrong we will not forget Jesus on the cross extending his forgiveness; so that when we are healed of an addiction we will return like the grateful leper and give thanks.

The main prayer by which we remember Jesus is the Eucharist. In this sacrament we hear the word of God and receive the Bread of Life. The Mass, our central liturgical prayer, holds us together as a community, bonds us to our ancestors, unites us to our God. As fewer Catholics attend Mass regularly, the memory of Jesus is endangered.

Prayer Draws All Into Christ

"Love is a many-splendored thing," as the song says. And so it is. Love not only makes the world go round, it is the most important gift that we can receive and give away. A loveless world is hell.

I propose that when we die and face God we will face one question, the question that Jesus addressed to Peter along the seashore: "Do you love me?" Our destiny hangs on our reply.

One of the primary places and times that love is offered to each of us is prayer. As we intentionally come into God's presence for serious conversation, we come into the presence of Love. Just as we cannot stay out in the summer sun for hours without being changed by the sun's radiation, we cannot abide in the presence of the Son without having our minds and hearts transformed by the mystery of grace, grace which we call love.

Saint Augustine once described grace using seven Latin words: "*Quia amasti me, Domine, fecisti me amabilem.*" "Because You have loved me, O Lord, You have made me lovable." Herein lies the power of prayer. Through the mysteries of creation and redemption we come to know that we are truly loved. The experience of God's love gives us the ability to love and to be loved.

Many people don't feel lovable, neither loved by others nor capable of self-giving. Life has dealt them a messy hand: Violence, discrimination and prejudice shatter their hope. They feel excluded from the circle of love. Prayer is a way for them to move into the circle of God's love and the community of the followers of Jesus.

Why does prayer draw us into union? How does this encounter with God bring love into our lives? Authentic prayer reveals to us the truth—the truth of God's love, the truth of our intrinsic dignity, the truth of our brokenness and sin, the truth of the Spirit who baptized us and confirmed us into a whole new life. Prayer rejects the lie that God is indifferent, that humans are intrinsically evil, or that we have been abandoned. Once we are exposed to the truth and see the darkness of falsehood, the possibility of experiencing love becomes real.

When love is present, there is unity. We see it at the kitchen table when family members respect one another.

We see it in our places of employment when people are dealt with fairly and with compassion. We see it in school when teachers and students honor each other in their common pursuit of wisdom. Love leads to community, joy and peace. Love is guided in the truth revealed in prayer.

Once, as a boy, I received a set of magnets for Christmas. I marveled that, placed one way, the magnets jumped and clung together. Pointed in the opposite direction, my small hands could not force them together. Prayer aligns the human soul to the mystery of God's love. Our whole life, with all its joys and sorrows, all its virtues and imperfections, is drawn into the heart of our Savior. What is of light is blessed; what is of darkness is cleansed. Prayer through love makes all things new.

Prayer Helps Us to Internalize the Liturgy

A duck's back sheds water so the feathered creature doesn't become waterlogged and unable to fly. But if we experience life as "water off a duck's back" we might well be accused of being incapable of deep experiences.

Prayer is a process of internalizing and assimilating. It is an attitude of openness before the mystery of God that allows the Divine Light to enter the deepest crevices of our soul. Bringing a prayerful disposition to liturgy, our public worship, fosters our union with God.

We've all heard the cry, "I don't get anything out of Mass." The waters of word and sacrament wash over us but never soak in. The gospel is proclaimed but our hearts do not stir. The host is elevated and we dream of the brunch later in the morning. We receive Christ in the

Eucharist and our emptiness only deepens. What's wrong?

Thomas Hardy, the melancholy British novelist, writes this about one of his characters: "She had sung without being merry, possessed without enjoying, outshone without triumphing." To experience the moment there must be an inner disposition of presence and openness if contact is to be made with the truth at hand. Prayer is that inner disposition. It takes us out of our subjective imprisonment and presents to us reality, the mystery of God. Thus prayer sets us free and empowers us to make our own the joys and source of life. Prayer connects us to the vine from whence all life comes.

Prayer can be blocked from doing its "job" by a number of obstacles. Here are three:

Preoccupation. If our minds are crowded by a thousand thoughts and our hearts are cluttered with a thousand desires, it will be extremely difficult to center on the liturgy. Prayer, employing the grace of silence, seeks to quiet the mind and still the heart in the hope of welcoming our "refugee" God. We must make room in the inn by means of prayer.

Subjectivism. One of our contemporary diseases is our failure to accept a reality totally independent of us. Liturgy is a corporate ritual that says: "God, transcendent and eternal, comes among us in the person of Jesus through the power of the Spirit." Whether we know it or not, whether we believe it or not, God is here—now. Prayer puts us in touch with the divine mystery and breaks down the theory that all reality is merely subjective.

Apathy. Not caring can be a way of life. An attitude of indifference creates paralysis and fosters a deep self-centeredness. Prayer, when undertaken with great seriousness, counters apathy by energizing us to hear and do God's word. More, when a prayerful attitude links us to the power of Eucharist, we are strengthened to do works of justice and mercy.

Effective prayer says: "I bring to Mass all that I am and have. I come away enriched and energized to further God's kingdom." Prayer internalizes and assimilates the liturgy and draws us into communion with God and with one another.

Prayer is hard work, but God always takes the first step. It is God's gift that we are able to pray. Because we are graced to share in God's life the yoke becomes easy to bear and the gift a source of joy.

Growing in Faith

- *Name the ways some common prayers tell you about the mystery of life.*

- *Are there ways that you see God revealed in your daily life?*

- *Why is memory so important to faith?*

- *How is prayer linked to love?*

Prayer in Practice

Six Ways to Pray

- *Each morning ask, "God, how can I do your will today?"*

- *In imitation of Jesus, do loving acts of kindness.*

- *Remember and reflect on ways that God has touched your life.*

- *Slowly and reflectively recite a prayer from your tradition, such as the Lord's Prayer or the Hail Mary.*

- *Pray a silent or vocal blessing before each meal.*

- *Prayerfully listen to your favorite religious music.*

CHAPTER FIVE

Our Father: A Spiritual Map

The art of mapmaking is a noble profession. Many people have been saved, thanks to the labors of a distant cartographer. Without knowledge of longitudes and latitudes we do get lost: lost in the woods, lost in fears, lost on the spiritual path. Fortunately there are people around—guides, teachers, spiritual cartographers—who shout out: "You are HERE!"

The *Catechism* is a map that charts for us our Godward life. It provides us with beliefs and practices that have been tested by Tradition. It guides us through the jungle of confusion that characterizes our culture. Our task is to study, understand and make our own the wisdom that keeps us from getting caught in dead-end alleys, that keeps us from getting lost.

Jesus came to save those who are lost. As our teacher and cartographer, our Lord has drawn us the supreme map for praying well: the Our Father. Since this is "the fundamental Christian prayer" (#2759), it is good for us to ponder each section to extract its wisdom and respond to God's call.

Map 1: Our Father...

Who is this God who dwells in heaven? The poet George Herbert laments that we humans spend so much time studying the things of this earth and so little time on the Maker of this creation. Prayer addresses this concern: "Our Father, who art in heaven, hallowed be thy name." We turn directly to God and, at the urging of Jesus, call God our Father. We further pray that God's name be honored and revered. "Thus the Lord's Prayer *reveals us to ourselves* at the same time that it reveals the Father to us [cf. *GS* 22, #1]" (#2783).

To call God Father means that we are God's children, daughters and sons, members of a single family. This revelation is astounding, its implications mind-boggling. What happens in Bosnia becomes a matter of family concern. What happens to welfare reform touches people in our own household. The fact that there are street people means that we have yet to take seriously our Christian responsibilities.

In *The Language of Life: A Festival of Poets* (Doubleday, 1995), TV journalist Bill Moyers interviews 34 poets about their work and life. One poet, Jane Kenyon, shares candidly her struggle with being a manic-depressive. She writes: "My belief in God, such as it is, especially the idea that a believer is part of the body of Christ, has kept me from harming myself. When I really didn't want to be conscious, didn't want to be aware, was in so much pain that I didn't want to be awake or aware, I've thought to myself, *If you injure yourself you're injuring the body of Christ, and Christ has been injured enough*."

What is God's name? Naming is a powerful and

dangerous activity. Powerful because it implies a certain level of knowledge and responsibility, dangerous because we might think that we have dominion over or control that which is named. Jesus instructs us otherwise. We are to hallow, reverence, honor the name of God, which comes to us through revelation. Since the mystery of God is so complex, we have been given multiple names: trinitarian names of Father, Son, Holy Spirit; theological names of Creator, Redeemer, Sanctifier; poetic names of Water, Fire, Wind.

In humility we come before the awesome mystery of God and cry out with Isaiah: "Holy, holy, holy." Perhaps we hallow God's name even more by kneeling in silent, loving adoration, aware that our inadequate speech is bound to fail. We further hallow God's name by living gospel lives, embracing the radical demands of the Beatitudes.

Map 2: Thy Kingdom Come...

Jesus used images to tell us about the Kingdom of God, images like a tree, a flock, a net. Pope Paul VI spoke of the Church as being universal, "a great tree whose branches shelter the birds of the air, a net which catches fish of every kind...a flock which a single shepherd pastures" (*Evangelii Nuntiandi*, #61). Whatever the metaphor, the truth is that God's reign and governance is to be worldwide, that the Kingdom of God is to come to all people.

The Church teaches that the Kingdom of God is essentially about peace, a peace that means rightness of relationships. But peace is possible only where there is truth, charity, freedom and justice.

The poet Gerard Manley Hopkins cries out that "piecemeal peace is poor peace." God's Kingdom comes when we speak and live the truth. God's rule is impaired when we lie and embrace the false. The *Catechism* emphasizes the truths of the dignity of the human person, the fact of sin and evil, the promise of redemption, the gift of the Holy Spirit and many more. When we listen, understand, assimilate, and then live these truths, God's reign has come upon us and light shines in the darkness.

God's Kingdom is about charity: sheltering the homeless, caring for the sick, forgiving sin, offering hospitality to the abandoned. Love is the core of the Christian message. Love must govern our lives if we are to become authentic disciples. Saint Paul helps to draw a portrait of God's Kingdom reflected in a life of love: Among God's people there is kindness and patience, no jealousy nor rudeness, no brooding over injuries nor rejoicing in wrong, no limit to truth or hope (see 1 Corinthians 13:4-7).

God's Kingdom is about freedom and justice. All of us struggle to be free—physically, psychologically, spiritually. Addictive thought patterns and behaviors block us from responding to God's subtle calls. The Holy Spirit has been given to us to set us free, especially from fear. That same Spirit impels us to do the works of justice, to be deeply concerned about promoting and protecting the rights of all. God's Kingdom is furthered as we fulfill our duties and obligations to God and one another.

On the feast of Christ the King the whole Church

prays (in the Preface to the Eucharistic Prayer) for "a kingdom of truth and life, a kingdom of holiness and grace, a kingdom of justice, love and peace." Jesus taught us to pray for this kingdom. What he began we are to continue by sharing, through Baptism, in his single mission and ministry. This map points us in the direction of a peace that is no longer piecemeal, but full and abundant.

Map 3: Thy Will Be Done...

What is the one commandment that summarizes the entire will of God? "Our Father 'desires all men to be saved and to come to the knowledge of the truth' [1 Timothy 2:3-4]. He is 'forbearing toward you, not wishing that any should perish' [2 Peter 3:9, cf. Mt 18:14]. His commandment is 'that you love one another; even as I have loved you, that you also love one another' [Jn 13:34, cf. 1 Jn 3;4; Lk 10:25-37]. This commandment summarizes all the others and expresses his entire will" (#2822).

Rabbi Harold Kushner, in the book *Who Needs God* (Summit Books, 1989), talks about his grandfather who lived in Lithuania and worked as a house painter. But Kushner describes his grandfather's secret identity: "He was one of God's agents on earth, maintaining literacy in a sea of ignorance and kindness in a world of cruelty." Is this not another expression of God's will for us: to bring truth and love into the world despite the darkness of ignorance and the disease of violence?

The prophet Micah proclaimed God's will in the often quoted passage about God asking but three things of us: "to do justice, and to love kindness, and to walk humbly with your God" (Micah 6:8). The difficulty arises at the kitchen table when a parent must discern whether or not grounding the teenager is the loving thing to do. Or, when an employer wrestles with whether he is acting justly, doing God's will, in releasing someone from her job.

Is it God's will that we embrace the darkness of doubt and the humiliation of despair as a part of divine providence? In general terms, God's will receives little argument. But it's a little trickier discerning the specific will of God in each of our lives.

Jesus faced the same difficulty. In Gethsemane, and also at the other two places of ultimate sacrifice—the Last Supper and Calvary—Jesus came face to face with the question of the Father's will. Scripture records the fear and the sweating of blood, the horror of approaching suffering. Yet Jesus held firm and proclaimed, even in the darkness, a radical yes to the circumstances that surrounded him. The knowing and doing of God's will is surrounded by risk and non-knowing.

Faith is essential here: "By prayer we can discern 'what is the will of God' and obtain the endurance to do it [Rom 12:2; cf. Eph 5:17; cf. Heb 10:36]. Jesus teaches us that one enters the kingdom of heaven not by speaking words, but by doing 'the will of my Father in heaven' [Mt 7:21]" (#2826).

Prayer is a faith posture. We come before God seeking insight and endurance. God has promised us the gift of the Spirit so that we have an assurance that in our attempt to follow Jesus we will be guided and strengthened every step of the way. Our American self-reliance must be set aside if we are to participate in the Paschal Mystery of Jesus' dying and rising. Gifted with the Spirit and supported by the Christian community all things are possible—even knowing and doing God's loving design.

Map 4: Our Daily Bread...

The hungers of the human heart are many. We long for meaning in a world that so often appears to be absurd. We thirst for a sense of belonging in an age of individualism. We search for depth in a culture of superficiality. Add to this list our hunger for authenticity, love and peace and we come to realize how needy we are: "Give us this day our daily bread." Our God addresses our needs: "The Father who gives us life cannot but give us the nourishment life requires—all appropriate goods and blessings, both material and spiritual" (#2830).

Our God is a giving God. This historical fact should instill in us trust, trust that God will continue to provide for our needs. So much of life and our limited energy can be wasted by senseless anxiety. Our prayer is one of faith and God is a God who is faithful.

There is an important social component to this petition in the Our Father. When we ask to give "us" our daily bread, we should be sensitive to the fact that often God will also give to others *through* us. As people come to us with their hunger for meaning and love, for depth and belonging, we must attempt to address those concerns inasmuch as we reasonably can. God's providence is often mediated through the community.

What is our daily bread? "'Our daily bread' refers to the earthly nourishment" we all need to live and also to "the Bread of Life: the Word of God and the Body of Christ" (#2861). Our lives depend upon two tables: the kitchen table where our bodies are fed and the table of the Lord where our souls find meaning in the Word and life in holy Communion. This eucharistic table addresses our deepest hunger, the hunger for intimacy and union with our God. Jesus himself becomes our food and drink, sharing with us his very life in sacrifice and feast. Already we are given a foretaste of heaven.

Thousands of children on our planet die each day because of malnutrition. Millions of people are starving to death in another way for want of spiritual nourishment. In prayer we come before our God with the urgent request that all the members of our human family might be given sufficient bread for body and for soul. If our petition arises from the heart we can be assured that it will be answered.

Map 5: And Forgive Us...

Prayer must deal with the dark side of life, sin. *Sin* has many levels of meaning: basic disobedience to God's command, the breaking of relationships causing hurt and guilt, the turning away from the God of light and choosing darkness. We stand in radical need of God's mercy: "And forgive us our trespasses, as we forgive those who trespass against us." In the words of the *Catechism*, "The fifth petition begs God's mercy for our offences, mercy which can penetrate our hearts only if we have learned to forgive our enemies, with the example and help of Christ" (#2862).

Two essential lessons for life, hopefully learned at the knees of our parents, are the lessons of "thank you" and "I'm sorry." Joyful gratitude for gifts received is basic to a Christian way of life. Joyful gratitude is one of the chief characteristics of a disciple of Jesus.

The second lesson: When we injure someone intentionally or through neglect, we need to ask for forgiveness before reconciliation is possible. This prayer that Jesus gave takes us into the heart of our human lives, the places where we love and hate, where we help and offend. We come before the God of mercy seeking healing, which means that we have assumed responsibility for our sins.

What are our trespasses? Disobedience to the law of love. We ask forgiveness for our failure to show concern for others, to respect their tempo and pace, to respond to their needs, whether spoken or implicit, to seek to communicate with them beyond a superficial level. Our trespasses? Breaking relationships by a sharp word, by excessive demands, by neglect. We even trespass against ourselves when we do not care for our minds and bodies through basic discipline. Our trespasses? Yielding to the attraction of darkness by watching TV programs that exploit sex or failing to object to violence that cheapens human life. We turn our backs on God and enter into the realm of chaos.

We need daily to pray for forgiveness. But be forewarned: We ask God to forgive us *as* we forgive others. We explicitly seek to be judged with the same ruler of mercy that we apply to others. The gospel story about the steward who was forgiven a large debt and then went out and throttled a fellow servant who owed him a small amount should make us shudder. Unfortunately the parables of Jesus too often apply to our personal lives.

Forgiveness, in fact, is beyond our human capacity. Without grace we are powerless. It is the Holy Spirit dwelling within us who empowers us to be healed and to become a healer. Because of Jesus there is light even in the darkness of sin, because from Calvary mercy has been extended to the whole world. Bathed in the waters of divine forgiveness, we are sent forth to share the reconciliation given to us.

Map 6: And Lead Us Not...

Temptations begin early in life. A child walking through a candy shop has a difficult time not pocketing a piece of chocolate. Later, the teenager hears a juicy rumor that is obviously inaccurate, but is tempted to pass it on for all kinds of reasons.

Later still, we adults are fascinated by prestige, power, possessions, productivity and pleasure. In and of themselves, these are all basically good, but within moments they turn from being means into *ends*. Making what should be means to a goal an end in itself can be a kind of idolatry. We can make a god of money or pleasure. Therefore we pray: "And lead us not into temptation, but deliver us from evil."

Grace is needed if we are to remain faithful to God's ways: "The Holy Spirit makes us *discern* between trials, which are necessary for the growth of the inner man [cf.

Lk 8:13-15; Acts 14:22; Rom 5:3-5; 2 Tim 3:12], and temptation, which leads to sin and death [cf. Jas 1:14-15]" (#2847). No one can avoid trials and temptations. In fact, the struggle between light and darkness, between good and evil, is a necessary ingredient in the formation of the human person. But we must not enter this area alone. We need the companionship and wisdom of the Holy Spirit.

In the Sacrament of Confirmation the prayer that accompanies the laying on of hands is rich in theology and powerful in describing the gifts necessary to withstand the temptations of life that lead to evil. The bishop prays: "All powerful God,...by water and the Holy Spirit you freed your sons and daughters from sin and gave them new life. Send your Holy Spirit upon them to be their helper and their guide. Give them the spirit of wisdom and understanding, the spirit of right judgment and courage, the spirit of knowledge and reverence. Fill them with the spirit of wonder and awe in your presence...."

The Our Father is a prayer for guidance by the Holy Spirit. The "leading" and the "delivering" is the work of the Holy Spirit. As Jesus led the people of his day into doing good and out of the darkness of evil, today the Spirit of Jesus continues that ministry. This petition is a request that our Confirmation in the Lord might be deepened.

Even today we are tempted to erect golden calves. We are especially susceptible to seeking our identity by what we have (possessions) or what we do (productivity) rather than by who we *are* inside. We tend to put too much value on our social status (prestige) and on what and whom we can control (power) than on the *virtues* of humility and obedience. And always we are attracted to comfort (pleasures) rather than the *sacrifice* that is part of the gospel mandate. Indeed, we must constantly pray, "Come, Holy Spirit, come," if we are not to yield to those idols which lead us directly into evil.

Although we may not think about it this way much, we live trinitarian lives: God is our Father and Provider; Jesus is our Redeemer and Friend; the Holy Spirit is our Sanctifier and Consolation. The Our Father relates us to this life. This prayer reminds us of who we are and what our Christian lives are all about. It is the foundational prayer of our faith.

Growing in Faith

- *What does the Our Father reveal to us about ourselves?*

- *Name an easy time of following God. Name a difficult time.*

- *Have you ever felt lost in faith? How did you find your way?*

- *What has the kitchen table meant in your life? The eucharistic table?*

Prayer in Practice

Litany of Thanks

Thank you, O Lord, for
creating me,
sustaining me,
loving me.

Thank you, O Lord, for the people in my life,
especially _____, and for the goodness of all
creation. May your will be done on earth as it is in
heaven.

CHAPTER SIX

Overcoming Prayer's Five Obstacles

Things get in our way! We plan a picnic but it rains. Conflicting work schedules get in the way of serious discussion between spouses. Past hurts block free communication between friends. If we are faced with hurdles in human dealings, should meeting some obstacles in our relationship with God surprise us?

In our prayer life, we can expect some difficulties and can't let them hinder us from raising our minds and hearts to God. In her book *The Measure of Our Success: A Letter to My Children and Yours,* Marian Wright Edelman offers twenty-five lessons for life. At the center of the pack is #12: "Never give up."

Zacchaeus could not see Jesus because he was too short and the crowds too large. Judas could not see Jesus because the money bag, a mere thirty pieces of silver, had taken over his heart. In his youth, Saint Augustine could not see Jesus because of unbridled sensuality. Our vision, too, can become myopic and dimmed by obstacles. The *Catechism* lists but a few of the potholes disrupting our prayer journey to God. We'll look at five: distractions, doubts, dryness, forgetting and acedia, the noonday devil of spirituality.

We need not become discouraged. The Holy Spirit is just around the corner—no, actually *within us* to help us surmount *any* obstacles as we strive to worship our God and serve our sisters and brothers. In all that we do we have a divine companion (and, we hope, a supportive community). We do not rely on our own limited gifts in responding to the call of discipleship. The Spirit prays within us, as Saint Paul reminds us, and the Spirit is able to deal with all the potholes, no matter how many or how deep.

Overcome Distractions With Attention

I have been in Grand Central Station only once, and that was enough. The volume of noise and the massive, moving crowds threatened to stifle my rustic heart. I longed for the quiet of the meadow lane. The experience of Grand Central Station can happen not just in New York but in the quiet of our bedroom or family den. We try to be alone with God but inside there comes a multitude of thoughts, noises, images. We find it hard to center, to focus on the presence of God who is with us here and now.

Or we may be at Sunday Mass when a baby's wail threatens to drown out the choir, or a small boy two rows ahead of us begins to beat up his third-grade sister or the server faints during the Eucharistic Prayer. Our spirit of loving attention to the things of God will certainly be interrupted at such moments.

And yet, distractions are a part of life. Our challenge is to deal with them in a reasonable and disciplined manner. Several suggestions come to mind. First, as we enter into prayer we do well to invoke the first verse of Psalm 70 as it is prayed in the Liturgy of the Hours: "O God, come to my assistance; O Lord, make haste to help me." As limited creatures reaching out to our infinite God, we realize the impossibility of the task without divine assistance, without divine grace. Handling our distractions just by ourselves will probably be a lost cause. Most of us lack the mental discipline to stay focused for more than eighteen seconds! God has promised to be with us at all times and surely God will be with us as we attempt to be open to divine revelation and to respond in prayer.

Second, maybe some distractions are not distractions at all. As we are driving home from work and saying a Hail Mary, suddenly we are distracted by the thought of a neighbor who is in the hospital a block away. God may be asking us to pay attention to this distraction, stop saying the Hail Mary and go to the hospital for a short visit. Another distraction may prompt us to ask forgiveness of someone we've hurt. Often God may get some agenda items on our To Do list by means of divine distraction in prayer. Of course, this does demand some discernment, some sorting out, because a distraction may well be an evil spirit drawing us away from our centering in God.

Third, distractions remind us that we are a pilgrim people and that all of us struggle. We straddle time and eternity. We are located between freedom and enslavement. We strive to do God's will while caught in our own willfulness. Distractions keep us humble. They make us more keenly aware of our solidarity with millions of people who strive to find God in a confusing world. This does not make the journey any easier and it does not allow us to ask for exemptions. Distractions, like the mosquitoes of summer, are here to stay. Happily, there are some benefits even from mosquitoes—ask the evening bats.

Overcome Doubt With Trust

We have certitude about death and taxes. Beyond that, everything may seem to be up for grabs, everything can enter the circle of doubt. Even the great saints at times questioned the existence of God.

Five major doubts surround us during our turbulent times: (1) doubt about the intrinsic goodness of human nature given the massive amount of cruelty and violence; (2) doubt about the providence of God in the face of the Holocaust and other horrendous massacres; (3) doubt about our capacity to know the truth in a world of pluralistic thought and radical subjectivism; (4) doubt about the afterlife in our absorption with the here and now; (5) doubt above love and fidelity as we witness a civilization of apathy and broken promises.

Coming to prayer in this atmosphere challenges us. God's word is hard to hear among hundreds of other voices shouting for our attention. Yet God *does* speak and all the doubts in the world cannot still the message of the Good News. Our faith always comes back to Jesus, Jesus crucified and risen. By focusing on the face of Jesus we see that God's love is real and active.

We trust in God's abiding presence and love. This trust enables us not to be paralyzed by the unknown, but to move forward in the dark with the assurance that we are being led by an invisible hand. Mary, the mother of Jesus, did not have certitude about what would happen to her. She lived in faith and trust in God. Indeed, the Holy Spirit overshadowed her, leaving no paralyzing doubt.

Doubt travels in a family system. Its cousins are muddled thinking, skepticism and relativism. Like a ball of yarn that we tug at, muddled thinking simply becomes increasingly raveled. Our thinking about ethical standards, about what is appropriate in personal relationships, about how to discern God's will can become confused. Prayer is a time of clarity. We come before the Lord to allow the divine word to shape our lives.

Overcome Dryness With Fidelity

Prayer is similar to the communication process between friends. We've all experienced periods of aridity or dryness in friendships. At times the dialogue between friends will be animated, filled with topics of interest and even humor. But then there are days and weeks in which not much happens: We feel no excitement, low energy and even a smidgen or more of boredom. This is normal. We can't live on a continual "high."

Periodic aridity and dryness in prayer is also normal. We think that prayer should be consistently "productive," well-watered and bearing much fruit. To be faithful when the field is fallow is an indication of deep belief. Here lies a paradox. We can continue to grow spiritually in subtle and silent ways at those moments when, from all appearances, nothing is happening. It's like the winter fields that lie dormant under the snow: that downtime is necessary for future abundant harvests.

Sometimes our prayer is dry, not because of the normal cycles of spiritual growth, but because of a lack of discipline or because of sin. Communication takes effort. It carries with it the price tag of attention. When we fail to do our part in raising our minds and hearts to God, we may experience the suffering of spiritual aridity.

When sin enters our lives, be it through disobedience to God's command or our breaking of relationships through neglect, our prayer life will be deeply affected. How would it be possible for prayer to be vibrant and flourishing when we have turned our hearts away from the source of life?

What should we do when our prayer is dry? Sometimes it is best to stay with the regular prayer routine we have and be as faithful as possible. At other times we might profit by varying the way we pray. Find a new hymn to sing to God, turn to a piece of poetry, sit down and talk to a friend or a spiritual director to discover what is and, more likely, what is not happening in our lives. If the invitation is simply to stay in the desert and be with the Lord in solitude and dryness, there we stay. If we are simply caught in a rut and need variety, then we seek some alternatives to enrich our conversation with God.

Whatever the cause for dryness, there is one thing that we must never forget. Charity is the core of

Christian living. Regardless of how well or how poorly our prayer is going, we can still reach out to others in active concern. The authenticity of our prayer life will always be measured by our love for our sisters and brothers in need. Jesus challenges us to love one another in a certain way, in the same way that he loved us. That is the way of total sacrifice, even unto death. No degree of dryness can prevent us from being concerned for others.

Back in high school many of us were forced to read Samuel Taylor Coleridge's long ballad "The Rime of the Ancient Mariner." Some of us can even recite from memory: "Water, water, everywhere...." But it was at the end of the ballad that we were given a deep theological insight that helps us to deal with the relationship between prayer and love:

> Farewell, farewell! but this I tell
> To thee, thou Wedding-Guest!
> He prayeth well, who loveth well,
> Both man and bird and beast.
>
> He prayeth best, who loveth best
> All things both great and small;
> For the dear God who loveth us,
> He made and loveth all.

We need but render some loving service to those who are in need and often our aridity and dryness vanish. Love waters our souls and keeps them from shrinking.

Jesus spent forty days in the desert. He spent some lonely hours in Gethsemane. And he spent an anguishing eternity on the cross, his lips parched and his soul in apparent spiritual abandonment. We do not experience aridity alone. Our God has been there before us and we must keep this in mind as we strive to persevere in deepening our relationship with God in all seasons, during time of drought as well as harvest.

Overcome Amnesia With Remembrance

The dictionary defines *amnesia* as partial or total loss of memory due to brain injury, shock, depression or fear. Amnesia is a huge pothole along the path of prayer. We no longer remember where we came from or where we are going. We no longer recall the countless miracles that surround us. We block out, often unconsciously, the abiding, loving presence of the Holy Spirit.

Some years ago I forgot the birthday of one of my friends. The friendship almost ended that day. No present, no card, no call: big-time trouble. We all know what this experience is like. Although it seems to be a small matter, anything to do with friendship has considerable weight.

Forgetfulness injures relationships and, when the loss of memory is total, the relationship is over. The question must be raised. Has our culture forgotten the mystery of God? When happiness is based on accumulating material possessions, competing for power, achieving pleasure in sex or drugs, God seems to be unnecessary, existing perhaps, but certainly on the fringe. In such an environment prayer becomes difficult.

The Second Vatican Council fostered spiritual renewal in powerful ways: emphasis on the Bible; retrieving much of our rich traditions; a profound liturgical renewal and so much more. But with every gain there is a loss. One of the consequences of the changes was a loss of our devotional life, those practices that helped us stay connected to God in between eucharistic celebrations. Such things as the rosary, novenas, the Angelus and litanies are now unfamiliar to a whole generation of Catholics.

These practices, though at times overstressed, did serve a major objective: They kept us mindful of our Godward life. They drew our attention to our business with God, the heart of our faith life.

We need to find ways to counter spiritual amnesia. For some people it will be reading a chapter a day from the Bible. For others it may be joining a faith-sharing group and bringing to the discussion how God works in one's life. Others may make a retreat, keep a journal or simply be sure to say meal prayers. A conscious effort is called for if we are not to have a severe memory loss of our God who longs to share divine life with us.

A wedding ring is a reminder of a promise and commitment. Even when spouses are separated by miles or years because of circumstances, the ring is a visible symbol of their commitment to each other. Removal of the ring can well begin a process of forgetfulness that can lead to infidelity. There are symbols all around us to remind us of our connectedness to God: the rainbow telling of an ancient covenant, the baptismal font where we began our life in Christ, the crucifix that recalls our redemption, even the gentle summer breeze reminding us of God's Spirit. Sacraments and sacramentals invite us to remember and respond in thanks and praise.

Spiritual amnesia is not just a minor illness. It can be terminal. Forgetting about God results in a loss of our humanity. We need but scan the evening paper to see what is happening in society as it suffers the loss of memory. We lose our human dignity when we lose contact with its Source. Prayer is a time to remember and to celebrate, to confess and intercede, to come back home to our Origin and our End.

Overcome Acedia With Rejoicing

Here is a strange word to modern ears. *Acedia* hearkens to medieval times, but its meaning is as relevant as ever. It is a disease not of the body but of the soul. Some of the symptoms are a loss of faith, a sense of futility, the loss of zest for life, an almost physical revolt against prayer, a constant state of dreariness. I recall a line from a short story that went something like this: "He didn't feel like going to sleep, he didn't feel like digging, he was tired of standing still, tired of lying down." When this illness falls upon us, our prayer life is in big trouble. The *Catechism* links several other characteristics to acedia: sloth, depression, joylessness, noonday devil.

Sloth and prayer are like oil and water: They don't mix. Although we might want to do most of our praying in bed, the chances of being present to God's word or of responding to it are rather minimal. Prayer demands attentiveness. We must be alert and disciplined in our conversation with God if we are to follow through on God's agenda that rises in prayer: Feed the hungry, tend to the suffering, welcome the stranger. Lazy people find this rather disgusting and begin to suffer acedia.

Depression is sometimes chemically caused. Good

medical care is advised. But sometimes our morale and spirits are down, way down, because we are not in God's good grace. In our more honest moments we must be willing to see the linkage between sin and some depression. Lack of harmony at our interior center can easily cast us into darkness and heaviness. Reconciliation, the prayer of forgiveness, is necessary to lift our spirits and reconnect us to God and the human community. Acedia demands more than a prescription for Prozac.

A retreat master became upset with the gloomy faces staring at him conference after conference. Losing his cool, he cried out: "For God's sake: Look redeemed!" Why is joylessness so pervasive within and outside the Church? One ancient writer claimed that joy is the knowledge that we possess something that is good. In prayer we constantly turn toward that good, God's life within us. Here is cause for great rejoicing. Here is how we drive that noonday devil, acedia, out of our land.

In Dante's *The Divine Comedy* the poet Virgil is leading Dante on a journey. Suddenly a sheet of fire blocks their path. An obstacle indeed! Fear of the fire paralyzes them. Then Virgil advises Dante to look through the fire into the eyes of his beloved Beatrice. Suddenly he is free, having shifted his eyes from the danger to the desire of his heart.

There will be many obstacles to prayer. But if we keep our eyes fixed on Jesus and trust in the Holy Spirit, they will draw us into deeper friendship and see us safely home.

Growing in Faith

- *How can distractions be good?*

- *How do you remember God daily?*

- *How does the Spirit pray within you?*

- *What is your most serious obstacle to prayer? Why?*

Prayer in Practice: Five Paths to Prayer

- *Pay attention.*

- *Trust.*

- *Hang in there.*

- *Remember.*

- *Rejoice!*

CHAPTER SEVEN

Prayer's Two Sides: Personal and Communal

Some things are inseparable. Inhaling and exhaling, for example: You can't breathe without doing both. Similarly, we need both personal prayer and communal prayer. Our prayer isn't really prayer without both. We can't do without either. Evelyn Underhill, the gifted Anglican spiritual writer, states it well: "...the praying Church is built of praying souls." Individual prayer is the foundation of the Church's public worship.

Two excerpts from Confirmation letters testify to the fact that people are at different places in their experience of prayer. One letter writer says, "I get nothing out of going to church. I sometimes talk to God at home. Even though my parents make me go to church, nothing happens inside. Why should I do something that doesn't change me?"

Another writes, "I like being with people and doing things together. Every Mass on Sunday is a special time for me. At our church the music is really good and the people are friendly. I can 'feel' God at times, especially when I go to Communion. I would be lost without the community and its support."

Our needs and styles vary, but we encounter God both in the privacy of our own heart and in the public arena of our lives. To exclude either is to be diminished because we cut in half our avenues of grace.

In this chapter we'll look at three key qualities of personal prayer: humility, charity and honesty; and three qualities of communal prayer: objectivity, support and solidarity.

Personal Prayer

A decade ago the National Conference of Catholic Bishops published a letter on the economy. In that document there was a single sentence that summarized a theology of work: "Work enables us to make a living, to exercise our gifts, to contribute to the common good and to further God's creative design." Thus, when someone is unemployed, we realize how devastating that can be for many reasons.

Prayer likewise enables us to nourish our spiritual life, to express our unique relationship with God, to enrich the broader community and to give God glory and honor. Prayer serves many functions and each one is significant.

No two souls are the same. Each one of us has different fingerprints, a unique history, diverse capacities, specific limitations and failings. God comes to us as individuals and our response is unlike that of anybody else. It is important to honor our personal rhythm and appreciate the different stages of growth that are part of our life story.

It follows rather naturally that moms and dads

bring to their prayer time family concerns; teachers might ask for the gift of wisdom or insight; farmers turn to the Lord in thanksgiving for a good harvest. Teenagers come with their questions and dreams; the elderly, with their memories and their diminishments. God takes us where we are and loves us deeply as we venture further on our faith journey.

There is a danger, however. Personal prayer can easily slip from being *individual* into becoming *individualistic* and eccentric, severed from any relationship to the larger community. Recent studies of our society describe the phenomenon of individualism and what it does to a nation and various societies within that nation. Two major consequences are a withering isolationism and a profound loneliness. A delicate balance must be maintained between our individuality and the whole body of Christ.

The Trappist monk Thomas Merton issued this warning:

> Individualism in prayer is content precisely with the petty consolations of devotionalism and sentimentality. But more than that, individualism resists the summons to communal witness and collective human response to God. It shuts itself up and hardens itself against everything that would draw it out of itself. It refuses to participate in what is not immediately pleasing to its limited devotional taste here and now. It remains centered and fixed upon a particular form of consolation which is either totally intimate or at best semi-private, and prefers this to everything else precisely because it need not and cannot be shared.

The *Catechism* notes three key qualities of personal prayer that will make it authentic and keep it from individualism:

Humility. "...[H]umility is the foundation of prayer. Only when we humbly acknowledge that 'we do not know how to pray as we ought' [Rom 8:26], are we ready to receive freely the gift of prayer" (#2559).

Again Thomas Merton is of help: "The gift of prayer is inseparable from another grace: that of humility, which makes us realize that the very depths of our being and life are meaningful and real only insofar as they are oriented toward God as their source and their end." How easily we forget our identity and our destiny. How easily we fall into worshiping false gods, the idols of power, prestige and possessions.

Humility is the grace that puts us in touch with the truth of things. All is gift. The humble person gives thanks. We are created and redeemed in Christ. The humble person gives praise for so glorious a Redeemer. We live in total dependency upon God, so we intercede for our needs and the needs of others.

Saint Catherine of Siena, a doctor of the Church, warns us of the dangers of pride, the antithesis of humility: "For all of the vices are born of selfishness because it is from selfishness that the principal vice, pride, is born. Those who are proud are bereft of any loving charity, and their pride is the source of impurity and avarice. Thus are these souls their own jailers, locking themselves up with the devil's chains."

Personal prayer, grounded in humility, fights selfishness and pride and thereby frees us from the prison that seals us off from the larger community. Humble, personal prayer leads to loving charity, the goal of our spiritual life.

Genuflection is one symbol of humility and a gesture of prayer. As we enter church and the presence of the Blessed Sacrament, we bend our knee to our loving God. Little things do mean a lot. Our genuflection and kneeling draw our bodies into prayerful reverence. Like making the sign of the cross, we are to make liturgical gestures with dignity and conscious intention. These symbols remind us to whom we belong.

Charity. "Love is the source of prayer; whoever draws from it reaches the summit of prayer" (#2658). Personal prayer, like all spiritual exercises, is done in the interest of love. If prayer does not come from a heart of love and if prayer does not eventually lead to union with God and unity with our sisters and brothers, we must question its authenticity. Prayer connects us to God, God who is love, and love transforms our lives.

One way to describe prayer is "love in action." In the famous Martha and Mary story (see Luke 10:38-42), we know that Mary's sitting at the Lord's feet was a prayer position. We must not forget that Martha too, in doing the details of hospitality, exercised her own unique form of prayer and respect—perhaps a little overdone, but prayer nonetheless.

The widow's giving so generously of her limited resources (see Mark 12:41-44) is a prayer of love. So, too, with the parent who sits up all night with a sick child, the funeral director consoling the family dealing with a suicide or the hermit who prays hour after hour for the well-being of the world. The widow gave her mite in love; the widow received Love in exchange. Not a bad transaction.

Honesty. "...[U]prightness in human action and speech is called *truthfulness*, sincerity, or candor. Truth or truthfulness is the virtue which consists in showing oneself true in deeds and truthful in words, and in guarding against duplicity, dissimulation, and hypocrisy" (#2468).

Fiddler on the Roof was popular for many reasons: good music, moving story, great acting. I enjoyed it because the main character, Tevye, was a man who had an honest relationship with God. He talked to God as a friend, as someone he could argue or laugh with, express his anger and affection. He came to God as he was, a struggling pilgrim, confused, excited, puzzled, grateful. Personal prayer demands honesty.

This virtue exacts a price. We have to shed our false self that we construct with so much effort and such subtle ingenuity. We hide behind security and achievement, degrees and possessions. Even our "goodness" can mask the deeper self that is rebellious and refuses to be guided by God's impulses. Not much happens in prayer unless we bring the real self to the living and true God. Not much happens without living in the truth.

Honesty is indeed the best policy in prayer, as in every path of life. There is no freedom unless our minds and hearts are grounded in truth. Personal prayer helps to link truth to morality. The great Hindu Mohandas

Gandhi shared his experience of truth and morality: "But one thing took deep root in me—the conviction that morality is the basis of things, and that truth is the substance of all morality. Truth became my sole objective. It began to grow in magnitude every day, and my definition of it also has been ever widening."

Communal Prayer

Personal prayer has a partner, the prayer of the community. We call this "liturgy," the public expression of our faith in word, song and gesture. We need both protein and vegetables to balance our diet. Likewise, prayer, alone and together, is a spiritual menu that nourishes our soul, the community and the world.

Three qualities underlie communal prayer, this communication with God that we do together:

Objectivity. "Prayer cannot be reduced to the spontaneous outpouring of interior impulse: in order to pray, one must have the will to pray. Nor is it enough to know what the Scriptures reveal about prayer: one must also learn how to pray. Through a living transmission (Sacred Tradition) within 'the believing and praying Church' [*DV* 8], the Holy Spirit teaches the children of God how to pray" (#2650).

A contemporary danger is a deep-seated subjectivity, meaning that something is real only if the individual experiences it. Reality depends upon my consciousness. Communal prayer challenges all that is merely subjective and proclaims a Reality independent of our personal thought. The liturgy goes even further. It awakens our narrow perception of what is real and connects us to a community and to a vast tradition. Worship keeps us in constant remembrance of the life, death and resurrection of Jesus as we journey annually through the seasons of the Church's life. Communal prayer expands our horizons and points us outward to the service of a hurting world.

C.S. Lewis once said something to the effect that what we see and what we hear depend on who we are and where we are standing. That's a piece of wisdom. Regardless of who we are and where we are standing, there are worlds out there. Miracles pass us by unless a faith community helps us to see and gives us a place to stand. Our personal prayer needs liturgical prayer for two reasons: to provide maps for our faith journey and to encourage us to live in God's world, in God's Kingdom.

Support. "The cup of the New Covenant, which Jesus anticipated when he offered himself at the Last Supper, is afterwards accepted by him from his Father's hands in his agony in the garden at Gethsemani, making himself 'obedient unto death.' Jesus prays : 'My Father, if it be possible, let this cup pass from me...' [Phil 2:8; Mt 26:39; cf. Heb 5:7-8]" (#612).

We know the details surrounding that prayer in that garden. Jesus was looking for support from Peter, James and John. They fell asleep. Jesus faced his hour of trial in the darkness, in solitude.

Perhaps the greatest mistake in life is to travel alone. When we fall, no one is there to help us up. We are social creatures and need one another not only for education and personal growth, but also in our journey toward God. When we're down in the dumps, the community carries us with their prayers of praise and gratitude; when we are given new life, the community joins us in celebration. Our communal penance services give us encouragement as we confess our sinfulness together.

Recently a young mother died. She, her husband and child were not churchgoers. A parish priest in the vicinity heard about the death and went immediately to the home to offer his condolences. He also offered the church and a funeral liturgy, if the family so desired. Here is an excerpt from the husband's letter after the funeral: "I hadn't donated to the church, helped out at the festival, given anything to the school.... I was just one stranger who walked in the door and said, 'My wife died, what do I do?' And they treated me like I'd been a member since the day I was born...."

Solidarity. "In the sanctorum communio [communion of saints], 'None of us lives to himself, and none of us dies to himself' [Rom 14:7]. 'If one member suffers, all suffer together; if one member is honored, all rejoice together. Now you are the body of Christ and individually members of it' [1 Cor 12:26-27]. 'Charity does not insist on its own way' [1 Cor 13:5; cf. 10:24]. In this solidarity with all men, living or dead, which is founded on the communion of saints, the least of our acts done in charity redounds to the profit of all. Every sin harms this communion" (#953).

Communal prayer fosters a strong sense of the common good. There are six basic principles in Catholic social teaching: (1) the life and dignity of the human person, (2) rights and responsibilities, (3) the dignity of work and the worker, (4) the value of family and community, (5) option for the poor and (6) solidarity. Prayer—personal and communal—is intimately related to justice. We live in solidarity with our sisters and brothers: All our spirituality is necessarily social.

In Luke's Gospel we are given the story of Zacchaeus. After his encounter with Jesus and promise of conversion, the words are spoken: "Today salvation has come to this house" (Luke 19:9). Note carefully that what happens in Zacchaeus's soul affects his whole clan. Praying together reminds us that we are all part of one family.

Our belief in the Mystical Body of Christ provides a foundation for communal prayer. Christ is the head, we are the members. The space program gives us an image that brings home the fact that we are a single human family: the famous lunar photograph of the earth-rise. We all belong to this small global village, having the same longings, the same sorrows, the same joys. Though we express our uniqueness in different languages and customs, we all are essentially of the same stock, members of God's family.

Striking the Balance

Henri Nouwen writes, "Without community, individual prayer easily degenerates into egocentric and eccentric behavior, but without individual prayer, the prayer of the community quickly becomes a meaningless routine."

There is a pervasive tendency in life to go to extremes, to set up the false dilemma of either/or. In some instances, life is a matter of either life or death, either good or bad. Often, however, balance is needed. It's a question of both/and. Individual prayer ensures that our hearts are engaged in our dialogue with God. The presence of community assists us when we wander and affirms us when we are on the right path.

Like breathing, which requires both inhaling and exhaling, prayer requires the balance between solitude and public expression. How strong is a chain? Schoolchildren learn that the answer lies in the strength of each link. How strong and deep is the prayer life of the Christian community? By now, you know where the answer lies: in the prayer of each individual member.

Growing in Faith

- *Why is prayer both communal and private?*

- *Name some ways in which you are a unique creation of God.*

- *Why should we avoid individualism in prayer? How do you do it?*

- *How does your prayer affect those around you?*

Prayer in Practice

- *Look up the Gospel reading for next Sunday's Mass (check your parish bulletin or missalette). Read the passage prayerfully, alone. Reflect on its meaning for your life.*

- *Find someone to share next Sunday's Gospel with. Read it to one another. Talk about its meaning. How are your conclusions or inspiration similar to or different from when you read the Gospel alone?*

- *Listen to the Gospel proclaimed to the community on Sunday. Reflect on how your parish community shapes the way God's word works in your life.*

Eight Ways to Be Happy

What is happiness? Ask Charlie Brown. In a cartoon he seeks the advice of Lucy who responds: "Happiness is having a convertible and a lake." She goes on to explain that if the sun is out you take a leisurely spin through the countryside. If it's raining, you put the top up on the convertible, go out to your lake, and watch it fill up with water.

As Charlie scratches his head in puzzlement at this philosophy, the great Snoopy, overhearing the conversation, simply walks over and kisses Charlie Brown on the nose. Readers are left to make their own judgment: Does happiness come from a convertible, a lake or a kiss?

We all pursue happiness. Some seek it in possessions, others in prestige or power, still others in pleasure. Do they find happiness at the end of the road? In the Declaration of Independence the founders of our country boldly state that everyone possesses inalienable rights: moral claims to life, liberty and the pursuit of happiness. The *Catechism* adds a point. A Christian's happiness, it observes, is linked to prayer to and our relationship with God.

Here are eight ways to find happiness along our

spiritual journey. If they were eight easy ways, I could retire rich tomorrow. But we'll see that the way to true happiness is the way of discipleship. It comes only with God's help and our cooperation.

1. Accept Who You Are

We have all known families in which a grandmother, father or aunt is the center of the clan, the one who holds things together. Now, step back and look at the big picture. In history, some cultures have held God at the center. Others, for various reasons, have placed the human person at the center of the universe. How does that affect human happiness?

One theory is that unless we accept that we are creatures, we cannot attain happiness. By nature we are bonded to our Creator. To cut ourselves off from the very Source of Life is to be thrown into extreme loneliness. We did not make ourselves. Yet, most of us have at one time or another attempted to play the role of God. There is something—call it pride, sin or sheer stupidity—that wants to deny our total dependency upon a loving God. "With creation, God does not abandon his creatures to themselves. He not only gives them being and existence, but also, and at every moment, upholds and sustains them in being, enables them to act and brings them to their final end" (#301).

Happiness, observes writer Father Gerald Vann, has another essential ingredient: creativity. Our vocation as human beings is to imitate our God in being life-givers. God's plan is that all might have life, life to the full. God calls each person and community to participate in the development of this creative activity that advances the Kingdom (#306).

Not to participate in becoming creative life-givers is to miss out on life, on happiness. In the end there are but two types of people: those who give life and those who take life. In the end there are only happy and sad individuals.

"Christian prayer is a covenant relationship between God and man in Christ" (#2564). It is in and through the understanding of this covenant that we come to know our creatureliness and hear the noble call to creativity. Our happiness is a covenantal reality, grounded in our loving relationship with God. Our happiness is realizing that we are being kissed on the nose by our loving God.

"Creator God, you who made us in your image and likeness, help us to rejoice in our creaturehood. Assist us at every moment to be creative, life-giving partners with you in your work of redemption and sanctification."

2. Seek Union With God

The fourteenth-century mystic Julian of Norwich, whose profound revelations led her to a deep union with God, asserts: "For until I am substantially united to him, I can never have perfect rest or true happiness, until, that is, I am so attached to him that there can be no created thing between my God and me."

The desire for union and oneness is universal. It even touches the animal kingdom. In the opening scenes of the Oscar-winning movie *Babe* there are two moments of separation: A small piglet is taken from its mother and puppies in a litter are dispersed to new owners. The movie portrays the animals grieving as the bond is severed between mother and offspring. Anyone with an ounce of compassion can sympathize with their loss.

We are made for intimacy, union with God and unity with one another. Much of depression and sadness stem directly from this broken oneness: What was meant to be one has been divided. Causes for the division? Perhaps willful choice, maybe circumstances of time and place, possibly sin. Whatever the cause, the consequence is unhappiness.

The *Catechism* is clear: "[T]rue happiness is not found in riches or well-being, in human fame or power, or in any human achievement—however beneficial it may be—such as science, technology, and art, or indeed in any creature, but in God alone, the source of every good and of all love" (#1723).

Prayer plays an important role in keeping us in touch with this reality. When we are alone in our room or gathered in public worship, we will hear again and again the voice of God calling us to the truth of things. In prayer we keep relearning the intrinsic value of every created good and are reinstructed in how much weight to give it. We will also be reminded again and again that God is the supreme Good and only by joining our will to the will of God can we experience true happiness.

"God of all creation, help us to treasure all your gifts: the rising sun, the open meadow, the face of a beloved, good health, yes, even the pains of life. Never let us prefer any gift over you, the Giver."

3. Take Gratitude's Test

G.K. Chesterton once commented that we are thankful for little Christmas or birthday presents but don't acknowledge the big gifts like our health or life itself. He asks: "Can I thank no one for the birthday present of birth?" And he knew well that thanking his parents was not enough. His existence was grounded in the mystery of God. Chesterton maintained: "The test of all happiness is gratitude."

Good parents teach their children magic words: "Please?" "Excuse me!" "Thank you." These expressions foster good relationships and give entrance into the land of happiness. Other phrases lead to unhappiness, to division and alienation: "Give me!" "It's mine!" "In your face!" Words have power.

Joyful thanksgiving characterizes the Christian life. As we address God in the Eucharistic Prayer, we say: "All life, all holiness comes from you." A felt awareness of being totally gifted plunges us into the mystery of God. We call this grace. Happiness is grace embraced.

Is gratitude on the endangered-species list? Have we lost the ability in our times to recognize the Giver behind our many gifts? How is it that we take so much for granted: our freedom, our friends, our very existence?

One cause may well be the absence of prayer. Meals are begun and ended without a blessing or a thanksgiving. We rise from sleep and return to it without turning to God. We make trips on hurried, dangerous highways presuming safety. When we lose awareness of our giftedness, we lose our joy.

"Thanksgiving characterizes the prayer of the Church which, in celebrating the Eucharist, reveals and becomes more fully what she is" (#2637). It is at the altar that we give thanks for "the birthday present of birth," for the gift of grace, for the privilege of being a participant in history.

> *"God of extravagant giving, teach us to take nothing for granted. May we thank you for every good gift: a friend's embrace, a summer ice cream bar, the smell of new-mown hay, the ability to walk and work, the opportunity to be with others in their suffering."*

4. Surrender Yourself

The Declaration of Independence asserts our right to pursue happiness, it does not make the claim that we are born to be happy. Stanley Hauerwas, noted scholar and writer, holds that we must embrace a truthful politics, one that teaches us to die for the right thing, not one that claims that we are born to be happy. Hauerwas further asserts that only the Church can be trusted with helping us to know what to die for.

In a recent issue of the British periodical *The Tablet*, Gerald O'Collins tells of a Bavarian farmer and his wife who were harboring a Jewish family being pursued by the Nazis. When the farmer indicated to his wife that their lives were endangered because of this action, the wife simply replied: "But why should we worry? We believe in Jesus' death and resurrection." She had it right. The Church had given her truthful politics.

Reflection on the mysteries of our faith guides us

into the true meaning of life. In contrast to seeing life as an extended time in Disneyland, the Christian perspective looks at life as sharing in the Paschal Mystery of Jesus.

Authentic prayer leads us along the gospel path to discipleship. Putting on the mind and heart of Jesus is a lifelong adventure involving an invitation to participate in the cross as well as the glory of the Lord. A philosophy of "born to be happy" finds it difficult to embrace the mystery of suffering. Prayer is essential both for an understanding of costly discipleship and for receiving strength to live it.

Prayer is ultimately self-surrender to whatever God asks of us, even a surrender unto death. The *Catechism* says of Jesus: "...in *his last words* on the Cross, where prayer and the gift of self are but one" (#2605). This self-giving fulfills God's plan of love and gains for us salvation. In prayer, we learn to die for the right thing; in prayer, that dying actually takes place.

> *"God of wisdom, show us the way of Jesus, the way of compassion, forgiveness and love. Give us a cause to die for, give us a reason to be happy. Show us the path that leads to eternal life."*

5. Learn to Hope

C.S. Lewis once raised the question whether or not we have the right to be six feet tall, have a millionaire as a father or enjoy good weather on the day of our picnic. His opinion is that we do not have a right to any happiness.

But we do have rights which for our humanity's sake need to be protected and promoted: the right to be treated with dignity, to education and housing, to work and to pursue happiness. But the right to pursue happiness must not lead to a sense of *entitlement*. Happiness lies more in the land of aspiration and hope.

The virtue of hope, the *Catechism* says, responds to the happiness God has placed in our hearts. Hope inspires our activities and keeps us from discouragement. Hope opens our hearts to "expectation of eternal beatitude" (#1818).

To a certain extent, happiness is in our control. By loving or withholding love we can make each other joyful or sad. By choosing self-giving over selfishness we see to the needs of others and the by-product of such generosity is peace and happiness. Prayer becomes the well-spring of that generosity.

"Lord God, send your Spirit of wisdom upon us. Help us to see that happiness is not a right but the fruit of living in union with Jesus."

6. Find Love's Hidden Ground

Writing from the Trappist monastery in Kentucky, Thomas Merton struggles to make plain the experience of happiness: "And the simple fact that by being attentive, by learning to listen..., we can find ourselves engulfed in such happiness that it cannot be explained: the happiness of being at one with everything in that hidden ground of Love for which there can be no explanation."

Getting in touch with the hidden ground within each one of us is an adventuresome journey. One way of doing that is journaling, carefully noting both things we observe through our senses as well as the movements of the Holy Spirit within, deep down in the hidden ground of Love.

Prayer is a significant means for getting in touch with our inner selves. This involves paying attention and disciplined listening. It takes no time to make this journey nor does it require academic theology. Rather, a smidgen of faith will do and perhaps a drop or two of hope. The hidden ground that Merton speaks of is contemplative prayer: "It is a gaze of faith fixed on Jesus, an attentiveness to the Word of God, a silent love" (#2724). It is the place where all are one and happiness can be experienced.

> *"Draw us, Lord, toward your life-giving water. Lead us to the hidden ground of Love where your Kingdom is being realized. Strengthen us anew to seek you in the deep-down things of life and to place all our hope in you."*

7. Join Your Work to God's

There are many parts to happiness: simple courtesy, a sense of gratitude, mutual respect and meaningful, satisfying work. Happiness must not be relegated to those times and activities that are outside the circle of labor. If such were the case, existence would be dreary indeed.

Work comes in many varieties: mowing the lawn,

defending a client, tending the sick, baby-sitting, instructing first graders, milking the cows. Any of these can be part of a good day's work. Any of these can be done cheerfully or begrudgingly. What we do and *how* we do it impinge deeply on happiness.

Prayer can transform our work. This is true both at the start and at the end of a project as well as in midstream. Doing all work in the presence of God changes everything. Saint Paul advises us "to live through love in God's presence." This is the salt, added to the expenditure of energy, that makes our work life joyful. A chief part of Christian happiness is to bring a spirit of prayer to every work situation.

> *"Creator God, we participate in your work of giving life and love to others. May our labors be pleasing to you. Give us your Spirit that we may do our work well and, if possible, with joy. May no duty be too small in its power to give you honor and praise."*

8. Consecrate Yourself to God

We speak of those who make the vows of poverty, chastity and obedience as living "consecrated lives." This is a unique consecration, but all of us, through Baptism and Confirmation, are consecrated to the Lord. And this is connected to happiness.

In the Mass, our supreme prayer, we continually renew our consecration to God by "taking, offering and sharing" ourselves as an instrument and channel of God's love and peace. The bread and wine we bring to the altar as well as our monetary contributions help to ritualize our dedication to the Lord, a dedication leading to supreme happiness. Indeed, we might ponder a proverb from India: "All that is not given is lost." Happiness lies in the full gift of self in imitation of Jesus on the cross.

It is in prayer that we hear the call to consecration and happiness. Abraham is a model: "When God calls him, Abraham goes forth 'as the Lord had told him' [Gn 12:4]; Abraham's heart is entirely submissive to the Word..." (#2570).

> *"Lord Jesus, we have been baptized and confirmed in your love. We long to share more deeply your life. Consecrate us in your truth; assist us in your mission. Do not let us live unconsecrated, wasteful lives."*

Happiness is an elusive reality. Charlie Brown knew this, as do we all. On our better days we know that the most important thing in life is relationships. But we are not alone. God not only creates but sustains and provides for our every need. Through prayer we are given both the vision and the strength to pursue God's kingdom, a kingdom that leads to happiness because it is a kingdom of truth, freedom and love. Happiness is possible even without a convertible and a lake!

Growing in Faith

- *Where do you find deepest happiness?*

- *Name some ways you are a partner with God in creation.*

- *In what way is our everyday work holy?*

Prayer in Practice

- *Pray aloud or silently, at mealtime or some other appropriate moment, one of the eight prayers in italics at the end of each section in this chapter.*

- *Keep a prayer journal for one week. Any notebook or paper will do, and you needn't spend a lot of time writing. Take time each day to write down things you are thankful for, needs that are in your heart and ways that God is speaking to you in your life. You may discover that keeping a prayer journal from time to time will help you to pray.*

CHAPTER NINE

Becoming a Eucharistic People

Why is the movie *The Wizard of Oz* so popular? A fear-filled lion, a brainless scarecrow, a tin man without a heart, a little girl and her dog Toto—why do these characters continue to fascinate millions?

Perhaps because we see something of ourselves in each of them. We long for courage yet are often afraid. We seek truth but bump up against our vast ignorance. We yearn to love but experience coldness of heart. And, like Dorothy, we are away from home and sense our exile.

There is another "movie" that's worth analyzing because it tells us a lot about ourselves. Let's call it *To Emmaus and Back* (see Luke 24). We all know the story. After Jesus' death on Calvary, his disciples experience tremendous agony and remorse. Two of them have left the city of Jerusalem and are heading home to Emmaus. On the way they meet another pilgrim and fail to realize that he is Jesus. But after a serious conversation and after the breaking of bread at table, they come to know that Jesus is risen. This Gospel story is about prayer and about our becoming a eucharistic people. The first step is to face ourselves honestly.

The Human Condition

The *Catechism* is clear: "Asking forgiveness is the prerequisite for both the Eucharistic liturgy and personal prayer" (#2631). On the road to Emmaus we don't see the disciples asking for forgiveness as such, but we do see them honestly admitting their discouragement and doubt. All their hopes had been placed in Jesus who was crucified. Everything they believed in seemed stripped away. Nothing was left.

I was once asked what part of the Mass I liked best. Immediately I thought of the distribution of Communion when people come forward to receive the Body and Blood of Christ. To witness their faith and reverence is a privileged moment.

I asked my questioner what part of the liturgy she liked best. For her it was the confession of sins. She went on to explain, "Getting in touch with the truth of our being, our humanness, our creaturehood, and knowing that Mary and the communion of saints are praying for us—well, it's a real high point in the liturgy for me."

Jesus encounters us in the Eucharist in this special moment of truth-sharing. Beneath our masks and social roles, we are essentially the same: creatures who are struggling to live good lives. And we all fail to some degree.

We come to Mass with our distractions and fears, our doubts and disappointments. We bring our good deeds and moments of joy, but we are also keenly aware that we have not responded to God's goodness as we ought and that we have often neglected others in their need.

This awareness is not all darkness. Facing the truth of our being always brings light. It is indeed not only a confession of sins that we are about, but also a confession of *faith*. We believe in God's mercy and help. We know in our hearts that we are loved and already forgiven. In this prayer we forge another link in our becoming a eucharistic people.

The great Hindu Mohandas Gandhi tells of a time when he deeply offended his father. His response was to make a clean confession to his father and, by so doing, the affection between them grew beyond measure. Gandhi adds that he made a promise never to commit that particular sin again. Repentance is the starting point in rebuilding any broken relationship.

We become a eucharistic people by building our relationship with God on the truth. Part of the truth is our brokenness and need for healing. Jesus takes us as we are, healing our wounds, and invites us more deeply into his intimacy.

Listening to the Word

Words have great power, especially the word of God. The Church tells us that "...prayer should accompany the reading of Sacred Scripture" so that a "dialogue takes place" between God and us (#2653). It is in the Liturgy of the Word that this serious conversation takes place: God speaking to our hearts and we, in turn, responding to the heart of God.

Jesus breaks open the Scriptures as he walks along with the two disciples. Starting with something they already know—the prophets and other books of the

Hebrew Scriptures—Jesus explains the meaning and how these sacred texts apply to his life and death. The words are spoken, understanding is given and lives are changed. Hearts that moments before were cold and forlorn now blaze with renewed hope and wisdom.

What happened here was prayer. Jesus spoke, the disciples responded. What happened here was new life in the face of death. What happened here was the formation of a eucharistic people.

We each walk our individual paths. Sunday after Sunday the word addresses us where we are on the journey, speaking in a unique way to our hearts. Our primary task is to listen with awe and wonder and then respond in obedience to whatever Jesus asks of us.

Some of us walk the path of fear, and God speaks through the prophet Isaiah: "Do not fear, for I have redeemed you; I have called you by name, you are mine" (Isaiah 43:1). Some of us travel the road of discouragement and sorrow. We are invited to hear God speak through Saint Paul: "Rejoice in the Lord always; again I will say, Rejoice" (Philippians 4:4). Others of us might find our hearts troubled, even ruptured: "Do not let your hearts be troubled. Believe in God; believe also in me" (John 14:1).

The call to community flows from our Baptism. We become God's people when we listen in faith and respond in love to God's redeeming word.

At Table With the Lord

Conversation, if serious and authentic, leads to communion. Prayer leads to intimacy and presence. Two large symbols speak to us of being a eucharistic people: the altar and the table (#1383). We gather in faith at the altar of sacrifice and the table of the Lord. Jesus himself is the victim offered for our redemption and Jesus himself is food unto everlasting life. We are indeed a blessed people.

Our movie, *To Emmaus and Back*, is only half over. The story continues. The stranger, giving the impression of moving on, is invited in for a meal. He accepts. At table he takes bread (*Offertory*), breaks it (*Consecration* and *Fraction*) and gives it to the disciples (*Communion*). Just as their ears were opened and their hearts caught on fire while on the road, now their eyes recognize the Lord in the breaking of the bread.

The whole scene is a moment of prayer, of encounter between God-in-Jesus and his people. Through word and symbol the covenant relationship is experienced with its transforming power. Things are now different. All is new. Discouragement turns to hope, doubt to faith, inertia to commitment. The disciples hurry off to proclaim the good news: God is with us, Emmanuel.

It is by mutual hospitality that we become a eucharistic people, God living in us, we living in God. This joint opening of hearts is at the core of our spiritual life. As guests of the Divine Host we are given great treasures, gifts such as wisdom, reverence, wonder and awe. As hosts of the Divine Guest we are to surrender ourselves to God's will. Prayer equates with hospitality, offered and received.

It is in the breaking of the bread that we participate deeply in the Paschal Mystery, the life, death and resurrection of the Lord. In Baptism we enter into the life of God; in the Eucharist that life is nourished and strengthened.

The road to Emmaus was not all that long; the road of life is. Often it is filled with deep anguish and suffering. We need to be fortified along the way lest we grow weary and discouraged. It is the grace and power of the Eucharist that empowers us to be faithful to the mission and ministry of Jesus, the work of teaching, healing, leading.

Back on the Road Again

The word *evangelization* is not easy to pronounce or spell. Nor is it easy to put into practice. Yet—and this may come as a surprise to many of us—evangelization is the Church's vocation, indeed, its deepest identity. The good news and the life in Christ that has been given to us is to be shared, both in word and in deed. This is the work of all baptized Christians.

The disciples who walked with Jesus on the road and broke bread at table were filled with joy, a joy they simply could not keep to themselves.

The Eucharist is not a "contained grace," limited to personal enrichment and devotion. Rather, it is love received that is meant to be shared. Thus the disciples could not sleep before conveying the good news to their companions back in Jerusalem. Even though night was falling, they were back on the road, hearts aglow, to tell others how their lives had been transformed. Simply put: Eucharist leads to evangelization.

It is joy that provides energy to do the work of the gospel. Mother Teresa of Calcutta was convinced of this:

Joy is prayer; joy is strength; joy is love; joy is a net of love by which you can catch souls. God loves a cheerful giver. She gives most who gives with joy.... A joyful heart is the inevitable result of a heart burning with love. Never let anything so fill you with sorrow as to make you forget the joy of Christ risen. (*A Gift for God*, Harper & Row, 1975, p. 77)

Prayer is linked to action. The word heard and understood seeks to be enfleshed in specific deeds and words. Jesus tells us to be generous. Thus, we go the extra mile, volunteer to help the poor, write out a check for the people in Rwanda. God's word calls us to compassion. So, off to the hospital, the nursing home, a homeless shelter. The Spirit prompts us to be reconciled. Therefore, we write that letter, asking forgiveness for a hurt we inflicted many years ago.

Evangelization is essentially the spreading of the good news of God's love in Jesus. In prayer we are invited to taste that love, in Eucharist we experience that love in profound intimacy. As evangelists each one of us has a special call to witness to gospel values, to make Jesus present in the circumstances of our life, to serve our sisters and brothers in need. The disciples, returning from Emmaus to Jerusalem, put into practice the truth they experienced in the Lord Jesus.

Sketch of a Eucharistic People

In most professional fields great stress is put on evaluation. Have the plans and objectives contained in the mission statement and plan been achieved or not? In our life in Christ, in being a eucharistic people, are there some standards by which to measure whether or not we are living lives of discipleship? The *Catechism* provides five benchmarks to help us assess our journey of faith.

A sense of wonder. "The wonder of prayer is revealed beside the well where we come seeking water: there, Christ comes to meet every human being. It is he who first seeks us and asks us for a drink" (#2560). We must never forget that our desire for God is nothing compared to God's desire for us. Francis Thompson, the poet, got it right. God is "the hound of Heaven" who pursues "down the nights and down the days." One of the great lessons of life is simply to stop all our hurrying and let God draw us into divine intimacy.

At Confirmation time we are reminded that one of the gifts of the Holy Spirit is wonder. We are surrounded by miracles. Our lives are permeated by grace. All we need are eyes of faith and hearts of hospitality. The great well where Christ encounters us is the Eucharist. Here it is that Jesus speaks to our hearts and enters our very being. We come away from the well, the Eucharist, nourished, a new people.

A sense of faith. Through Jesus we have intimate access to the Father and the gift of the Holy Spirit. In fact, "[f]aith is a filial adherence to God beyond what we feel and understand" (#2609).

The Eucharist invites us into a life of faith. Here we are attentive to God's majesty, adhere to Jesus as Lord, abandon ourselves to the slightest prompting of the Holy Spirit. As a eucharistic people we are a trinitarian community, relating to our God as Creator, Redeemer and Sanctifier. In the Mass God is revealed to us and we are revealed to ourselves. In the Mass we know to whom we belong.

Faith is imperiled today because of individualism, secularism, pragmatism. Despite these forces we still find people who are not overcome and who live deeply the word of God. Rabbi Abraham Heschel maintained: "We cannot live by a disembodied faith." We demonstrate our faith and overcome its obstacles by enfleshing our faith in loving deeds. In other words, the life of faith is as much about what we do as what we believe.

A sense of thanksgiving. Thanksgiving focuses upon God's many gifts: creation, salvation, the Spirit, the Church. As the *Catechism* says, "Thanksgiving characterizes the prayer of the Church which, in celebrating the Eucharist, reveals and becomes more fully what she is" (#2637). Our challenge is to take nothing for granted but to appreciate every blessing that comes our way. Thanksgiving is a whole way of life. Indeed, the prayer of thanksgiving characterizes a eucharistic people.

One of the measures of maturity for young and old is the capacity to say thank you. Our gratitude in a particular way centers on the greatest gift of all, the very person of Jesus. This gift, and all the other gifts that come our way through God's gracious providence—gifts like health, a good home, freedom, educational opportunities—are expressions of God's concern and love for us. How fitting and just it is that, in the words of the Eucharistic Prayer, we "always and everywhere" express our gratitude to the Lord.

A sense of commitment. Everyone remembers the judgment scene in Matthew's Gospel. Jesus tells us that whatever we do to one another, we do the same thing to him. It is true in feeding or withholding food from the hungry, in visiting or not visiting people in prisons and nursing homes, in accepting or turning our back on strangers.

In Baptism we make promises. In the Eucharist we are given strength to keep promises. A line from Phyllis Rose's *Parallel Lives* haunts me: "What does the promise of a permanent commitment mean when everyone knows it's provisional?" Our baptismal and eucharistic promise is not provisional. It is a commitment that is permanent in nature and eternal in significance. It obliges us to work for justice: *"The Eucharist commits us to the poor.* To receive in truth the Body and Blood of Christ given up for us, we must recognize Christ in the poorest..." (#1397).

A sense of the centrality of the Eucharist. As we look at the other sacraments and at all of our ministries and apostolic works we see that they are connected to the Eucharist in a powerful way: "The Eucharist is 'the source and summit of the Christian life' [*LG* 11]" (#1324). In other words, everything is centered on the person of Jesus and derives its meaning and power in connection with him. The vine and branches metaphor is a constant reminder of this fact.

Things in life take on meaning in the context of their origin and destiny. As human beings, our ethics and moral behavior stem from two deeper questions: who are we (our identity) and where are we going (our destiny). The Eucharist is the source and summit of our faith life. Around the table and altar we bring our joys and sorrows, our hopes and disappointments, our goodness and sinfulness. With and in Christ, the good is blessed, the darkness forgiven. Then off we go, down the road, toward the next assigned duty of our life.

Little Dorothy and her dog, Toto, ventured off to the land of Oz only by way of a strange nightmare. In point of fact, they never left the plains of Kansas. Our faith journey is no dream. It is a real, serious and dangerous adventure. In taking the road to Oz with her dog, the tin man, the lion and the scarecrow, Dorothy has given us a good lesson: Never travel alone.

As members of the faith community we journey together, relying on one another for support and encouragement. But we are not merely a human community offering mutual assistance. Our center is the person of Jesus whom we encounter so dramatically in the Mass. When we enter into this sacrament with deep faith and trust we will indeed become God's people, compassionate, loving, forgiving.

Growing in Faith

- *How is the Emmaus story a Eucharist story?*

- *Describe an "Emmaus experience" in your life.*

- *Why are truth and healing important in relationships?*

Prayer in Practice

- *For one week, end each day with an examination of conscience, prayerfully reflecting upon the events, conversations and activities of the day. Where is there need for healing in your life?*

- *Perform an act of charity this week for someone you know or for a stranger. Then read and reflect on Matthew 25:31-46 and the Emmaus story, Luke 24:13-35.*

CHAPTER TEN

The Heart of Discipleship

Would you be comfortable if they etched on your tombstone: "Here lies a disciple and steward of the Lord!"? Perhaps many of us might find these terms rather strange and yet, through Baptism, all of us are invited to follow the way of Jesus (discipleship) and to live in such a way that we treat everything we are and have as being entrusted to us (stewardship).

There are other possibilities for tombstones: "Here lies a hoarder...or a prodigal...or a glutton!" Names can characterize our lives and indicate the decisions that shape our destiny.

The *Catechism* consistently reminds us that prayer is necessary for our self-understanding. It is before the Lord, whether in solitude or liturgy, that we know that we belong to God and hear Jesus' call to embrace his values and vision. Through discipleship we consecrate our hearts to Jesus; through stewardship we accept the fact that we are accountable for the time, talent and treasure God continues to bestow on us.

Batterrrr up!

To score a run in baseball the runner must touch all four bases. Sandlot kids learn this really fast. By way of analogy, the disciple and steward of Jesus must also touch four bases to merit that marvelous affirmation, "Well done, my good and faithful servant [steward]!" (see Matthew 25:14-30).

First base: Receive God's gifts gratefully. All is gift: life, health, freedom, energy, colors, the blue moon, even sauerkraut (with dumplings). Every breath we breathe, every second of the hour, every ounce of affection is grace. Unfortunately, there is a big-time problem: We take things for granted. We have developed a mentality of entitlement and have become a demanding culture. In such an environment there are few thank-yous. We tend to forget the Giver.

The *Catechism* is most helpful here: "Prayer is the life of the new heart. It ought to animate us at every moment. But we tend to forget him who is our life and our all" (#2697). And if we forget our Creator, we become confused about creation and what it means. Even more, we become confused about who (and whose) we are.

In prayer we wake up. We become sensitive to the Grace (Love) behind all our blessings and graces. God tells us in prayer that we are responsible for tending the earth, for caring about the little people, for reverencing all of life from the womb to the tomb. A lack of prayerfulness makes us numb and blind to the many benefits of life. When prayer is part of our daily routine, our minds and hearts turn frequently to the God of abundant goodness, offering praise and thanksgiving for all God is and does. We become a eucharistic people, a thankful people.

British writer G.K. Chesterton offers an exercise that keeps us attuned to God's many gifts and helps us not to take things for granted:

> It is a good exercise, in empty and ugly hours of the day, to look at anything, the coal-scuttle or the bookcase, and think how happy one could be to have brought it out of the sinking ship on to the solitary island. But it is a better exercise still to remember how all things have had this hairbreadth escape: Everything has been saved from a wreck. (*Orthodoxy*, p. 64)

Pause for a moment and look around you. The hour need not be empty or ugly. Simply thank God for all the gifts that you have right now, all the gifts saved from the wreck of life: the lamp that illumines this page, the chair that gives you comfort, the home that provides shelter. That's a good exercise of stewardship indeed.

Another exercise: Practice saying "thank you" twenty times a day. Thank God for the food in the refrigerator, for the sun and stars in the sky, for the support of friends, for the opportunities of a new day, for the ability to laugh and cry. A disciple/steward receives everything with gratitude. It is prayer that helps keep the heart grateful and filled with joy.

Second base: Tend, nurture and cherish God's gifts responsibly. Saint Paul speaks eloquently of the diverse gifts distributed among the members of the Body of Christ. Each of us has the task of naming those gifts and becoming responsible for their development. How tragic it is when a person has an I.Q. of 120 and refuses to nurture that intelligence. How sad when a human heart is capable of deep love yet withholds that grace from others. Few tragedies are greater than a wasted life.

A key word comes into play here—a word that for many is considered a dirty word: *discipline*. Without discipline we fail in our discipleship and stewardship. How is it that one of the most popular books during these past fifteen years, M. Scott Peck's *The Road Less Traveled*, devoted one-fourth of the text to the issue of discipline? Millions of people have appreciated reading Peck's book because they know that the less-traveled road of love cannot be taken without serious discipline.

Without discipline, talents are not nurtured and developed. And a talent unused becomes a dangerous thing. The German poet Goethe puts it this way: "What is not used is but a load to bear." Could it be that a considerable amount of depression is a direct result of failed stewardship? To have a gift and not exercise it weighs us down. It affects others because they are deprived of a gift that God wants to come to them through us. Our call is to conversion, a spiritual discipline that cherishes and nurtures God's gifts in our lives.

Catholic Worker founder Dorothy Day understood conversion as a falling in love with God, which in turn frees us to reach out to those who suffer and are in pain. Stewardship involves this falling in love with God. It involves recognizing that what has been given to us is to be used with great responsibility. In other words, "Being a disciple is not just something we do, alongside many other things suitable for Christians, it is a total way of life and requires continuing conversion." So say the U.S. bishops in their 1993 pastoral letter *Stewardship: A Disciple's Response* (#14).

Conversion and discipline are first cousins and are inseparable. The *Catechism*, in speaking about the Our Father, states: "...[I]f we pray the Our Father sincerely, we leave individualism behind, because the love that we receive frees us from it" (#2792). It is God's love that frees us; it is grace that gives us the power to use God's gifts with great responsibility.

Third base: Share God's gifts justly and charitably. Sharing is another name for love. For disciples of Jesus, this sharing takes on a certain quality: sharing one's whole mind, soul and heart. Anything less is wanting in generosity.

We all have convictions. Here is one that captures well this third dimension of stewardship: "I unreservedly and with abandon commit my life and destiny to Christ, promising him practical priority in all the affairs of my life. I will seek first the Kingdom of God and his righteousness." This mission statement expresses the essence of stewardship: a sharing based on justice and love. The Lord does ask a lot, as the rich young man found out in the Gospel (see Matthew 19:16-22).

Two adverbs modify this sharing, the third element of stewardship: *justly* and *charitably*. Justice is rather straightforward: Give to God and all people what is their due. In justice we pay fair wages for services rendered, prepare class so that the students' right to learn is ensured, protect and promote human life at every stage. Justice is grounded in rights and duties.

Failure to be a just person or a just community is more than a want of stewardship. It is a failure in our very humanity.

More, much more than justice is required of Jesus' disciples. Thus we have a second adverb: *charitably*. This means going the extra mile without thinking twice, giving not from our surplus but from our need, living sacrificial lives with joy. Frugality has its merit, but not when it comes to loving. Jesus asks us to imitate his love by giving our very selves.

Every loving parent knows from experience what sharing charitably is all about. Sitting by the bedside through the night during times of illness; working an extra job to get the kids through college; forgoing personal desires because of children's needs. Countless people live lives of profound stewardship.

Depending upon personal circumstances and the commitments of life, each person and community must intentionally decide what is just and charitable. No easy task! For some people it may be one percent of their income and two hours of service a week. For others, 15 percent and five hours of service may be what the Lord is asking. The key thing is to take the first step in faith. God loves a cheerful giver.

If not enough money is coming into an individual parish or diocese or there seems to be a lack of participation in the life of the Church, it is not really a financial problem or lack of talents—it is a *faith* problem! Those who really believe that all is gift will respond by sharing God's gifts with justice and in charity.

An old adage still rings true: "Having too much is as dehumanizing as having too little." Not to share justly and charitably is injurious to one's own spiritual and human well-being. It is also injurious to the common good and the future of our world.

Home plate: Return God's gifts abundantly. God can never be outdone in generosity. That is the basic principle of stewardship. The more we give, the more room there is to receive new gifts from God to be given away.

Saint Irenaeus (from the second century) tells us that the glory of God is the human person fully alive. Disciples/stewards are fully alive when they receive, nurture, share and return God's gifts in abundance. We witness to this abundance when we feed the hungry, give shelter to the homeless, take in the stranger. Our return cannot be measured by the criteria of financial portfolios. It will be measured by the size and texture of our hearts.

The image of the harvest speaks of abundance. Jesus often expressed concern that laborers (read stewards) were too few in number. Such is the case today. God's purposes are imperiled if we fail to make an appropriate return of our gifts to the Lord. God calls us to be agents of divine love and mercy, called to address all the needs of the human family.

A summary statement of stewardship: a grateful reception of God's gifts, their responsible development, a just and charitable sharing of them and so an abundant return of them to the Lord. In prayer, we have the opportunity to evaluate how we are doing as God's stewards and as Jesus' disciples.

Stewardship and Prayer

Prayer is a constant reminder that all we are and have comes from the Lord. In a unique way the Eucharistic Prayer at Mass explicitly states that God is the origin of life and the source of our freedom. As we bring our gifts to the altar, we express our indebtedness and attempt to make an appropriate return to the Lord. Celebrating with reverence and awareness, we grow as disciples and stewards of the Lord.

Prayer leads us to an ever-deeper understanding that stewardship is essentially about self-giving. This awareness moves us beyond the giving of time, talent and treasure. When we imitate Jesus in his total self-giving, we experience the peace that is the consequence of obedience to God's will. In prayer we continually return to that call.

Prayer gives us a new perspective by which we see all life as a gift. Some writers speak of Mary as the model for all stewards: She saw all things, her duties, her sufferings and her joys, equally as gifts from God. Her motto, "let it be with me according to your word" (Luke 1:38), is a prayer of eternal significance. When we emulate Mary's gratitude and generosity, we know that our prayer is truly authentic.

Prayer is pragmatic—it works! It is because the Spirit prays within us that we are able to translate gospel values into deeds of justice and kindness. To attempt to be stewards on our own or even with the help of the community will ultimately be futile. We need the power of the Holy Spirit to rise above our pettiness and self-centeredness in order to be for and with others as Jesus was. Without prayer, a life of stewardship will not last.

Prayer provides an opportunity for assessment. Coming before the Lord at the beginning and end of each day, we can ponder together how well we use the gifts God has given us. Stewardship, after all, involves accountability. In the silence of prayer we are challenged to evaluate honestly how well we are sharing our time, talents and treasure. In the silence of prayer we are confronted with the ultimate question: Are we doing God's will or our own?

The Garden Question

The Spanish poet Antonio Machado raises a basic question in one of his poems: "What have you done with the garden entrusted to you?" This is the stewardship question. We must put it in plural and present tense: "What are we doing with the gardens entrusted to us?" Here is a brief examination of conscience which should be undertaken only in the environment of prayer.

Physical garden. Reverence for the body is fundamental for a healthy, happy and holy life. The stewardship questions in this area are: Do we take an appropriate amount of time for exercise and rest? Do we respect our sexuality? Do we eat properly and watch our weight? If our prayer life is holistic, we will hear God calling us to care for our bodies. A fit and healthy body contributes to both happiness and holiness.

Social garden. No one should travel alone. We are members of a human family and are intimately linked to one another. In faith, we are members of the body of Christ and we share one another's joys and sufferings. Perhaps the predominant illusion in the Western world is the presumption that we are autonomous. Prayer calls us to tend to the well-being of every needy sister and brother. Social stewardship demands that we confront the social evils of our day such as starvation, civil wars, ethnic cleansing, racism.

Political garden. Not only is no one an island but every person is part of the *polis*, the city. We are members of planet earth whether we live in the outback of Alaska or the inner city of Chicago. As citizens of a nation, we are challenged to be concerned about the common good and make our contribution to it. We tend well our political garden by assuming certain responsibilities: voting, being informed about issues and candidates, contributing to the public debate. Our stewardship is related to all political systems.

Psychological garden. Daniel Goleman's book *Emotional Intelligence* points out that we are challenged to be not only rationally smart, but also emotionally smart. Our I.Q. is important; so too our E.Q., our emotional quotient. We are stewards of our emotions and our affective life. By naming and managing how we express our feelings we grow psychologically and often spiritually. Much of human life involves interpersonal dealings, expressions of concern, the need for sensitivity and empathy. Through prayer and stewardship we must attempt to align our emotional life with God's purposes.

Cultural garden. The body needs proper nutrition to

remain healthy; the soul needs the enrichment of good music, literature and art. My grandmother's insight remains with me to this day: "What we get next to gets inside us!" Reading the poets, going to an art exhibit, visiting the museum—all these activities enrich our spirit. These are gifts from God that need stewarding. These are special graces to make us human.

Stewardship is a way of life, an expression of discipleship. Stewardship is a vocation that embraces many things: life, health, material goods, our natural environment, our cultural heritage. Our duty and privilege is to be good stewards of all the Lord has given to us. By so doing we find our greatness and bring glory to God.

Growing in Faith

- *Which of God's gifts do you value most?*

- *How do you nurture and develop your gifts?*

- *Name some ways that God calls you to share your gifts.*

Prayer in Practice

Here is a good prayer for all people desirous of living a life of stewardship:

> What shall I return to the LORD
> for all his bounty to me?
> I will lift up the cup of salvation
> and call on the name of the LORD,
> I will pay my vows to the LORD
> in the presence of all his people. (Psalm 116:12-14)

CHAPTER ELEVEN

Praying the Beatitudes

Bookends set limits for the books on our library shelves. They give us support and keep our precious books from tumbling down. Matthew's Gospel has bookends in Chapters Five and Twenty-Five. They give us a vision of our Christian life and a means of assessment. In the fifth chapter we are given the Beatitudes, our Lord's understanding of happiness. In Chapter Twenty-Five, the Last Judgment scene, we are depicted as sheep and goats that are separated according to whether or not we fed the hungry, clothed the naked, visited the imprisoned.

The *Catechism* highlights the importance of the Beatitudes: "The Beatitudes depict the countenance of Jesus Christ and portray his charity. They express the vocation of the faithful associated with the glory of his Passion and Resurrection..." (#1717).

By praying the Beatitudes with faith and in the sure knowledge of the Spirit's enlightenment, we can come to a clear understanding of who we are and what we are to do in following the way of Jesus.

Blessed Are the Poor in Spirit

"Blessed are the poor in spirit, for theirs is the kingdom of heaven." *Poverty* is a tough word. We war against poverty because having too little dehumanizes us (just as having too much does). Millions of people do not have the basics of life, thereby facing the possibility of death and tragic suffering. The poverty of misery is not only not condoned by the Scriptures, it is to be eradicated.

When Jesus speaks of poverty it is from a different point of view. People are blessed who acknowledge their radical dependency upon the Lord and live with an awareness that all is gift. Our fundamental human indigence points to our need for God and to the fact that nothing material can completely satisfy us. The poor in spirit live with a consciousness that every single moment is grace; they live with an abiding sense of gratitude for the smallest gift.

Thomas Merton expressed this type of poverty: "We do not want to be beginners. But let us be convinced of the fact that we will never be anything else but beginners all our life!" Or listen to Ruth Burrows: "Failure to accept the innate poverty of our condition leaves us dominated by anxiety." Or Dorothy Day: "Poverty is a strange and elusive thing...I condemn poverty and I advocate it; poverty is simple and complex at once, it is a social phenomenon and a personal matter. Poverty is an elusive thing, and a paradoxical one."

Prayer: "Gracious God, teach us how to be poor in spirit, always aware of and relying on your presence and power.

Strengthen us to fight against all poverty that destroys hope and life; give us courage to embrace the poverty that binds us to you and that refuses to fill up on wooing words, false securities, things that kill our inner spirit."

Meditation: *"To ['little ones'] the Father is pleased to reveal what remains hidden from the wise and the learned [cf. Mt 11:25]. Jesus shares the life of the poor, from the cradle to the cross; he experiences hunger, thirst, and privation" [cf. Mt 21:18; Mk 2:23-26; Jn 4:6-7; 19:28; Lk 9:58] (#544).*

Blessed Are Those Who Mourn

"Blessed are those who mourn, for they will be comforted." We mourn when we suffer loss: loss of a loved one, loss of a relationship, loss of innocence. To our contemporary ears it seems strange to call people blessed when they mourn. Would it not be more accurate to say: "Depressed are those who mourn, for they have suffered some severe loss."

But Jesus has a different vision. Someone who understood this was Jane Kenyon, who died at age forty-seven. One of her poems, entitled "Let Evening Come," was recited at her funeral. The poet describes in a beautiful way how the day ends and how darkness covers the earth. In all of this the refrain is: "Let evening come." Then, at the end, Jane Kenyon encourages the reader not to be afraid because God will never leave us comfortless. She spoke from personal experience.

On a quiet morning we might hear the plaintive song of the mourning dove. Its melancholy is haunting.

Perhaps the song might be interpreted: With every loss there is a gain; with every suffering, a new possibility of deeper compassion; with every deprivation, a hollow is made for the holy. Loss can be redemptive or nonredemptive. Faith whispers to us that there will always be the grace of comfort since God is with us in all the circumstances of our life.

Prayer: *"Loving God, when health fails and failures come, when friends are far away and days are dark, come to our aid with your consoling touch. Teach us the deep joy of your presence that is abiding and sustaining even in the darkest of times. May our blessedness bring happiness to others who suffer, too."*

Meditation: *"The beatitude...invites us to purify our hearts of bad instincts and to seek the love of God above all else. It teaches us that true happiness is not found in riches or well-being, in human fame or power, or in any human achievement...but in God alone, the source of every good and of all love"* (#1723).

Blessed Are the Meek

"Blessed are the meek, for they will inherit the earth." Webster's dictionary speaks of meekness in terms of people who are tamely submissive, easily imposed on, even spiritless. In Jesus' lexicon we find a different perspective. Those who are meek will be happy and they will inherit the earth. It's important to have more than one dictionary on the shelf.

The hero or heroine of our times is the willful person, the individual or community that does its own will, come what may. Jesus came proclaiming a gospel of obedience, if you will, a gospel of submission or meekness. *Submission* simply means being *"under"* the *"mission"* of another. In his case, Jesus was submissive to the will of God and instructed us to put on his heart, one that is meek and humble. Obedience seems to attack the democratic ideal of freedom, though in fact, freedom is gained only through submission to God's design. The path of peace lies along the way of obedience.

In Shakespeare's tragedy *King Lear*, the king's two older daughters professed great love for their father and in return received half the kingdom. As one would say, they inherited the land. The youngest daughter Cordelia refused to speak of love as a commodity and was banished from the kingdom without a dowry. In the end we see that Cordelia, the meek one, did inherit her father's love whereas the two older sisters lost not only the kingdom but also their lives to violence, lust and greed. Shakespeare's drama—and ours—is the moral choice between submission and willfulness.

Prayer: *"Lord Jesus, show us the humble, meek path of obedience. Free us from the pride that pits our wills against your own. Enable us to accept the joys and sufferings of life as part of your plan."*

Meditation: *"The Word became flesh* to be our model of holiness.... *Jesus is the model for the Beatitudes and the norm of the new law: 'Love one another as I have loved you' [Jn 15:12]. This love implies an effective offering of oneself, after his example" [cf. Mk 8:34] (#459).*

Blessed Are Those Who Hunger and Thirst

"Blessed are those who hunger and thirst for righteousness, for they will be filled." *Righteousness* is a long word, abstract and somewhat forbidding. Yet it has something to do with "right" relationships: families living in harmony, nations respecting one another, the human person and God on good terms. Unfortunately, there is much disorder in our world as well as in our hearts: broken treaties, manipulation and exploitation of the poor and powerless, widespread starvation, war and genocide.

Some people hunger and thirst for justice and peace. Call them prophets, mystics, teachers, social workers or whatever, their hearts are longing for right order. Many of them are willing to go to strange cultures and live with the poor, or stay in the inner city and strive for solidarity, or kneel in a monastery and pray for the conversion of the world. Some people are so filled with graced empathy that they cannot sleep well at night, knowing that their sisters and brothers are in want and pain.

Jesus instructs us that satisfaction is in store for those who hunger and thirst for righteousness. We might read into this that if we hunger and thirst for other things—possessions, prestige, power—there will remain a deep dissatisfaction in our hearts, a restlessness that leads to ceaseless experimentation. Only when we pursue a justice that leads to peace will we find authentic happiness. "To act justly," to seek righteousness, is foundational to discipleship.

Prayer: "Spirit of the living God, help us to see all humanity as part of our concern. Transform our indifference into commitment, our apathy into enthusiastic love, our lethargy into a rich sensitivity."

Meditation: "The virtue of solidarity goes beyond material goods. In spreading the spiritual goods of the faith, the Church has promoted, and often opened new paths for, the development of temporal goods as well" (#1942).

Blessed Are the Merciful

"Blessed are the merciful, for they will receive mercy." When the Pharisees condemned the disciples for picking and eating grain on the Sabbath, Jesus rebuked them and stated that God's desire is for mercy and not sacrifice. We need to be reminded of this time and time again since our culture is so dominated by attitudes of vengeance and recrimination. We desire mercy for ourselves but often find it difficult to extend it to others, especially in the face of grave, unrepentant injury.

Shakespeare's Portia had a wisdom about mercy:

The quality of mercy is not strain'd.
It droppeth as the gentle rain from heaven
Upon the place beneath. It is twice blest:
It blesseth him that gives, and him that takes.
(*The Merchant of Venice*, IV, I, 182-183)

Jesus' beatitude on mercy follows that of justice. Jesus made it clear that both mercy and justice are necessary for happiness. Again our friend Portia: "And earthly power doth then show likest God's / When mercy seasons justice."

Mercy looks like Jesus hanging on the cross when, in

131

the midst of incredible pain, he prays for his persecutors. Mercy looks like a father or mother welcoming home a son or daughter who has gone through all the inheritance, material and spiritual. Mercy looks like God's extravagant love wiping away forever every vestige of sin and guilt.

Prayer: *"God of mercy and justice, reveal to us the secret of your compassion and love. Give us strength to be gentle and firm, to be merciful and just. May your name be glorified by our deeds of mercy."*

Meditation: *"Instructing, advising, consoling, comforting are spiritual works of mercy, as are forgiving and bearing wrongs patiently. The corporal works of mercy consist especially in feeding the hungry, sheltering the homeless, clothing the naked, visiting the sick and imprisoned, and burying the dead [cf. Mt 25:31-46]. Among all these, giving alms to the poor is one of the chief witnesses to fraternal charity..."* (#2447).

Blessed Are the Pure in Heart

"Blessed are the pure in heart, for they will see God." Back in Chapter One, readers were challenged to memorize a four-line prayer by Dag Hammarskjöld:

Give me a pure heart—that I may see Thee,
A humble heart—that I may hear Thee,
A heart of love—that I may serve Thee,
A heart of faith—that I may abide in Thee.

Hammarskjöld knew about the Beatitudes. The connection between purity of heart and seeing God was an instruction that Jesus articulated for us with force and clarity. When our hearts are polluted, whether by pride or greed or lust or envy, a blindness sets in that prevents us from seeing God's graciousness and the beauty of our sisters and brothers. By contrast, when our hearts are transparent, our eyes are blessed with a compassion and sensitivity that pick up the presence of God in the darkest of circumstances.

Everyone struggles with purity, that virtue that pertains to all human experiences insofar as they are appropriate and fitting. While including human sexuality, it reaches far beyond it. The interior purity of the Beatitudes gives us joy that softens our gaze, sensitizes our ears and makes our soul holy. As the great theologian Romano Guardini once wrote: "Entirely pure, unweakened by evil, he was loving and open to the core." Impurity closes us off to reality.

Prayer: *"Loving God, give us purity of mind, heart and body. Assist us in tasting all life in accord with your will, thereby living in your peace."*

Meditation: *"The sixth beatitude proclaims, 'Blessed are the pure in heart, for they shall see God' [Mt 5:8]. 'Pure in heart' refers to those who have attuned their intellects and wills to the demands of God's holiness, chiefly in three areas: charity [cf. 1 Tm 4:3-9; 2 Tm 2:22]; chastity or sexual rectitude [cf. 1 Thes 4:7; Col 3:5; Eph 4:19]; love of truth and orthodoxy of faith [cf. Titus 1:15; 1 Tm 1:3-4; 2 Tm 2:23-26]. There is a connection between purity of heart, of body, and of faith" (#2518).*

Blessed Are the Peacemakers

"Blessed are the peacemakers, for they will be called children of God." God's daughters and sons are called to be peacemakers. There is another option: becoming instruments of division and chaos. Whether we look at the international situations with wars all over our planet, or into our homes and churches and institutions, indeed, into our hearts, we find an absence of peace. Hatred is chosen over love, darkness over light, despair over hope. Jesus came to bring us God's peace, another word for the Kingdom.

Peace has four satellites: truth, charity, freedom and justice. Although it is dangerous to modify the words of Jesus, we might expand the seventh beatitude to read: "Blessed are the truth-makers, the love-doers, the freedom-bringers, the justice-keepers. These are the members of God's family who sit around the divine table in joy."

Shakespeare knew of what he spoke in *Henry V*: In times of peace we humans assume modest stillness and humility. But come the blast of war, and we become as brutal as the tiger. Jesus knew of what he spoke: only the making of peace brings about the Kingdom of God.

Prayer: *"God of peace and joy, guide our journey of life along the paths of peace. May we speak the truth in the face of lies, may we love in times of hatred and indifference, may we free the oppressed and downtrodden and do justice toward all."*

Meditation: *"Injustice, excessive economic or social inequalities, envy, distrust, and pride raging among men*

and nations constantly threaten peace and cause wars.
Everything done to overcome these disorders contributes
to building up peace and avoiding war" (#2317).

Blessed Are Those Who Are Persecuted

"Blessed are those who are persecuted for righteousness' sake, for theirs is the kingdom of heaven." There's an old expression, "Where the rubber hits the road!" At some point we are all tested in our Christian lives. Can we still claim that we are disciples of the Lord when sufferings come? Saint Paul is the great model here when he claims that absolutely nothing can separate him from the love of God made manifest in Jesus: not even shipwrecks, beatings, nakedness or the sword.

The gospel promises no rose garden, no easy life. We are given the promise of presence, a presence that will sustain us when trials and tribulations rain down upon us. Through God's power we will be able to respond like Jesus in his hours of darkness: forgiving those about to kill him, extending mercy to his betrayers, comforting others in the midst of his own pain. The path has been cleared through the forest; our task is simply to follow.

This beatitude makes an important point. Persecution can come down upon us because of self-inflicted wounds. The persecutions spoken of in this beatitude involve those who endure for the sake of righteousness, for the sake of truth and justice. Again it is Saint Paul who says that there is no comparison between present sorrows and future glory; the glory so transcends persecutions that it's really no contest.

Prayer: *"God of strength and hope, may your kingdom come regardless of the price we must pay. Strengthen us with your Spirit of fortitude that we may say yes to the crosses you share with us."*

Meditation: *"The kingdom will be fulfilled, then, not by a historic triumph of the Church through a progressive ascendancy, but only by God's victory over the final unleashing of evil, which will cause his Bride to come down from heaven [cf. Rv 13:8; 20:7-10; 21:2-4]" (#677).*

Growing in Faith

- *Which beatitude challenges you most? Why?*

- *Name a time when God's presence has comforted you.*

- *What is the difference between being meek and being tamely submissive?*

Prayer in Practice

Read Chapters 5, 6 and 7 in Matthew. Each day, pray one of the eight prayers that accompany each beatitude in this chapter.

CHAPTER TWELVE

Nine Prayer Companions

L ast week a college senior shared with me her experience of doing a thirty-day Outward Bound program. A whole month in the wilderness! Two things made a deep impression on her: how we can survive on so few things (one change of underwear!) and the importance of companions.

In our faith life we don't need a lot of things but we do need good companions. These are the individuals, living or dead, who share their experience and share in ours. Some call these companions friends, soulmates or community. The underlying message is not to travel alone, for the road is long and it's easy to get lost.

If Henry David Thoreau was correct—"A man [woman or child] needs only to be turned around once with his [or her] eyes shut in this world to be lost"—we are well advised to surround ourselves with a company of saints and sages, a band of prophets and poets, a handful of witnesses of God's gracious love and mercy. The *Catechism* holds up for us a number of companions in faith. After commenting on five of these companions I will suggest several other companions whose writings and experience might enrich our pilgrimage of faith.

Companion of Faith: Abraham

What was Abraham's prayer? "The prayer of Abraham and Jacob is presented as a battle of faith marked by trust in God's faithfulness and by certitude in the victory promised to perseverance" (#2592).

A contemporary story of faith was in the newspapers not long ago. A baby fell from an apartment window and was amazingly saved from death when its diaper caught in a tree branch. As the branch bent low to the ground, the baby plopped to the ground unharmed. A maintenance woman who witnessed the event exclaimed to a reporter, "The hand of God reached out and saved that little baby!" That's seeing through the eyes of faith.

Faith is many things: accepting and living God's word as Abraham did; trusting that no matter what happens, God will be with us with providential love and support; surrendering our agenda to the concerns of God. Faith is a living, demanding relationship that is grounded in commitment and acceptance. It is an attitude of mind and heart that centers us on God.

Faith is difficult today. Indeed, faith can be lost. Our culture tells us that there is nothing beyond time and space. There is no eternity. As the ad says: "You only go around once. Grab as much as you can get." The word for this is *secularism*.

Faith is difficult because of so many different belief-systems (pluralism) and so many different theories about morality (relativism). Shakespeare's Hamlet, though speaking four centuries ago, articulates what many people believe: "...for there is/nothing good or bad, but thinking makes it so." We have lost a sense of objectivity and the importance of clear standards.

Like Abraham we must ask for the grace of faith. It is a gift to be received and virtue to be exercised. Like any other habit, unless we use it, it tends to diminish and die. Spiritual reading and conversation, daily prayer, communal worship, fasting and doing works of justice, are ways in which we keep in touch with a God who surrounds and sustains us. With Abraham we journey to lands unknown and to mountains of sorrow and deep joy.

Companion of Intimacy: Moses

"From this intimacy with the faithful God, slow to anger and abounding in steadfast love [cf. Ex 34:6], Moses drew strength and determination for his intercession. He does not pray for himself but for the people whom God made his own" (#2577).

There is room in the land of spirituality for formal, structured prayer. But when all is said and done, it is prayer arising from the heart that leads to intimacy and oneness. Moses is a model of one who knew God face-to-face. Moses' prayer was honest: "he balks, makes excuses, above all questions" (#2575). Here is a real relationship! He acted as a go-between, as one who accepted the difficult role of leadership in a period of history that was traumatic for his people, the Israelites. What sustained him was the grace that flowed from his conversation with the Lord.

Intimacy often develops "through a series of shared experiences on a dangerous journey" (Alan Moorehead). That's exactly what happened between God, Moses and the people. Their journey from slavery to liberation was dangerous and often discouraging. Their shared experiences involved great suffering and many heartaches. The end result was a bonding that led to a new identity in a new land.

Prayer and intimacy share many common elements: friendship and love, collaboration and negotiation, and yes, compromise and conflict. Intimacy and prayer are hardly romantic experiences. Rather, they demand a hard-nosed approach to life and relationships. The cost yields high results: an abiding peace and a holy joy. These signs of the Holy Spirit guarantee that the intimacy experienced is authentic.

Companion of Repentance and Conversion: David

"David is par excellence the king 'after God's own heart,' the shepherd who prays for his people and prays in their name. His submission to the will of God, his praise, and his repentance, will be a model for the prayer of the people" (#2579).

To journey with David is an interesting adventure. Here was God's chosen one, yet one who had to face his own sinfulness (murder and adultery) with brutal honesty. We learn from David the secrets of repentance and conversion. He takes ownership for his wrongdoing and comes to the Lord with a humble and contrite heart.

Prayer will always contain an element of conversion. Dorothy Day gives us a beautiful reflection on her experience of conversion: "a falling in love with God that frees us to reach out to those who are in pain." Prior to conversion we are caught up in ourselves. Subsequent to God's working within us, we are free to be with and for others. This conversion touches every dimension of our lives: the political and social, the cultural and economic, the spiritual and the moral.

Many of the most beautiful prayers of the Church, the psalms, are attributed to King David. These songs are about praise and thanksgiving, petition and repentance. Psalm 51 is the classic psalm of repentance and has spoken eloquently of our need for God's mercy:

> Have mercy on me, O God,
> according to your steadfast love;
> according to your abundant mercy
> blot out my transgressions.
> Wash me thoroughly from my iniquity,
> and cleanse me from my sin. (Psalm 51:1-2)

King David's company points us in three directions: honesty, humility and hope. David faced the truth of his own sinfulness and was set free: He donned the garments of humility and removed the false robes of arrogance. He found that God was faithful to divine promises and thus he could hope. Anyone who points us in this direction and goes that way with us is a great companion.

Companion of Loving Adherence: Jesus

"Jesus' filial prayer is the perfect model of prayer in the New Testament. Often done in solitude and in secret, the prayer of Jesus involves a loving adherence to the will of the Father even to the Cross and an absolute confidence in being heard" (#2620).

The centrality of Jesus in our prayer life cannot be overstressed. It is in and through Jesus that we come to the Father and live in the Spirit. Jesus reveals the mystery of God to us and is himself the presence and manifestation of God's love, mercy and compassion.

One of baseball's greatest players was Henry Aaron. When he broke into professional baseball in spite of many obstacles, he began to make a fairly good salary. He told his mother that he would like to buy her a new home. She said she wasn't looking for a new home, she was looking for Jesus!

And once we have found Jesus (or he us) our prayer life takes on a whole new dimension. Saint Paul is a primary example here. For him Christ was living and praying within his soul. Thus, when Saint Paul felt weak he knew that he was strong because the power of Christ's Spirit was working within him. One of the great resources we have in companioning with Jesus are chapters fifteen through seventeen in the Gospel of Saint John. There is sufficient material here to nourish us for a year plus eternity.

Companion of Joy: Mary

"Because of Mary's singular cooperation with the action of the Holy Spirit, the Church loves to pray in communion with the Virgin Mary, to magnify with her the great things the Lord has done for her, and to entrust supplications and praises to her" (#2682).

One of our beliefs as Catholics is in Mary's Assumption into heaven, a feast we celebrate on August 15th. Part of our tradition has been to turn to Mary to intercede for us in our special needs and the needs of the world. With deep faith, millions of people over the years have prayed the Memorare:

> Remember, O Most gracious Virgin Mary, that never was it known that anyone who fled to thy protection, implored thy help or sought thy intercession was left unaided. Inspired by this confidence I fly unto thee, O Virgin of virgins, my Mother. To thee I come; before thee I stand, sinful and sorrowful. O Mother of the Word Incarnate! Despise not my petitions, but in thy mercy hear and answer me. Amen.

Mary knows our human condition; she can identify with our human journey. Fear and ignorance troubled her sensitive soul when the angel came at the Annunciation. Anxiety and grief swept through her heart when Jesus was lost in the Temple, when he faced the cruel death by crucifixion. Mary has been there. Joy surged through her being as she visited Elizabeth who also was with child. Mary is one of us. She understands the road we all travel.

There is another prayer of Mary that continues to echo down the corridors of history, the prayer we call the Magnificat, in which Mary's soul magnifies the Lord for all the marvelous things that God did for her (see Luke 1:46-55). It is this prayer of praise that captures the essence of Mary's life: a life of total submission to a loving, merciful God. Mary continues to accompany us, a pilgrim Church, as we strive to be faithful to a God who has called us into covenant.

Companion of Adoration: Evelyn Underhill

Evelyn Underhill (1875-1914), a great spiritual author in the Anglican tradition, wrote extensively about spirituality and prayer. Her emphasis consistently was on the mystery of God who calls forth from each of us awe and wonder. Her integrated approach to the spiritual life always balanced prayer with action, adoration with practical love of those with whom we work and live, work with leisure, and study with specific ministry.

You might want to add to your library Evelyn Underhill's *The Ways of the Spirit* (Crossroad, 1993). "Prayer covers all ways in which our will and love reach out to one Reality and Love in adoration, longing, patience, confidence, and joy" (page 77).

Companion of Presence: Abraham Heschel

"What marks the act of prayer is the decision to enter and face the presence of God. To pray means to expose oneself to Him, to His judgment" (Abraham Heschel).

Abraham Joshua Heschel (1907-1972) is one of the leading spokesmen in the Jewish community regarding prayer and our life in God. Prayer for him is to see the world from the point of view of God and results in shifting the center of our lives from self-consciousness to self-surrender. Two things are essential: inner participation of the heart and the living of the word heard in prayer.

One of the conditions for prayer is a kind of silence that is much more than the absence of noise or sound. Rather, this form of silence is an absence of self-concern and an inner stillness that empowers the one who prays to be drawn deeply into the presence of God. It is a silence that disposes us to become attuned to God's slightest whisper or prodding.

Another volume for your spiritual reading list: Heschel's *Man's Quest for God* (Scribner's Sons, 1954). Some reflections from this great writer: "We dwell on the edge of mystery and ignore it" (page 4). "To worship is to rise to the higher level of existence, to see the world from the point of view of God" (page xii). "We have bartered holiness for convenience, loyalty for success, love for power, wisdom for information, tradition for fashion" (page 150).

Companion of Reality: Thomas Merton

"We don't want to be beginners. But let us be convinced of the fact that we will never be anything else but beginners, all our life!" (Thomas Merton).

Thomas Merton (1915-1968) reminds us that in matters of spirituality God is always in charge. We never really become masters or professionals in the prayer life. Each day is a fresh beginning and we come before the Lord in our nakedness and emptiness. And the Lord takes us just as we are and loves us again into being.

Merton, a Trappist monk for twenty-seven years until his accidental death in 1968, is a good companion because he relates spiritual insights so well to our everyday life. He speaks to the human condition and understands the human heart. His own failures and sin gave him a rich compassion and a great understanding of sin and guilt. One of Merton's deepest goals was to find out his true self and to bring his authentic self before the Lord.

In *Contemplative Prayer* (Doubleday, 1969), Merton writes: "Study plays an essential part in the life of prayer" (page 79). "Prayer then means yearning for the simple presence of God, for a personal understanding of his word, for knowledge of his will and for the capacity to hear and obey him. It is thus something much more than uttering petitions for good things external to our own deepest concerns" (page 67). "My true identity lies hidden in God's call to my freedom and my response to him" (page 68).

Companion of the Present Moment: Jean-Pierre de Caussade

"Our single duty is to keep our gaze fixed on the master...and to be constantly listening so as to understand and hear and immediately obey...." (Jean-Pierre de Caussade)

Jean-Pierre de Caussade (1675-1751) offers us a very simple rule in living a life of prayer. All we have to do is take each moment as it comes to us, accomplishing whatever it is the Lord wants us to do. Our task is to remain simple and pliant and responsive to the word of God. All this assumes a deep faith and trust that the Lord surrounds and sustains us. This French Jesuit truly believed that God spoke to us directly and we are to respond moment by moment.

What is the secret of the saints? "Did those saints of old have any other secret than to become each moment of their lives God's instrument?" (page 70). With the eyes of faith we are to see each moment as a sacrament of God and respond to it with courage and joy.

So here we have another volume for the spiritual journey: Jean-Pierre de Caussade's *The Sacrament of the Present Moment*, translated by Kitty Muggeridge (Harper & Row, 1966). More nuggets of wisdom: "This discovery of divine action in everything that happens, each moment, is the most subtle wisdom possible regarding the ways of God in this life" (page 91).

Prayer begins and ends in love. God is Love and it is God who draws us into the divine presence and sends us forth to live that love. We will pray well if we love; we will love well if we pray.

Growing in Faith

- *Who has influenced your faith most? Why?*

- *Who is your favorite saint or biblical figure? Why?*

- *Have you ever inspired someone else? How?*

Prayer in Practice

Peace Prayer Attributed to Saint Francis

Lord, make me an instrument of your peace;
where there is hatred, let me sow love;
where there is injury, pardon;
where there is discord, unity;

where there is doubt, faith;
where there is error, truth;
where there is despair, hope;
where there is darkness, light;
and where there is sadness, joy.

O Divine Master, grant that I may not so much
seek to be consoled as to console;
to be understood as to understand;
to be loved as to love;
for it is in giving that we receive,
it is in pardoning that we are pardoned,
and it is in dying that we are born to eternal life.